hey mama

IN CHRIST, YOU ARE MORE THAN ENOUGH

hey mama.

When I was expecting my firstborn, I was enamored with the "new name" that motherhood would give me.

I often stood in front of my bathroom mirror and "tried it on" like a new pair of jeans. Mommy.

Did it fit me? Did it flatter me? Did it feel right?

As I said the name aloud, I would study my own reflection and imagine that the woman staring back at me would be everything the name implied — patient and kind, servant-hearted and wise. Whimsical and wonderful and fun.

However, when my son finally arrived, I discovered that my "new name" didn't come with an instant "new me."

I was still impatient and imperfect, selfish and flawed. And as the days turned to weeks and weeks spiraled into months, that name began to feel more like a heavy weight than a badge of honor.

On most days, the name Mommy no longer felt like a shining statement of who I was; instead, it was a glaring reminder of who I wasn't.

The me in the mirror felt more sapped than super. The me in the mirror wondered how her soul could feel so empty when her hands were so full. The me in the mirror lay in bed at night, too weary to sleep, worrying if she was messing up her kids or disappointing her husband. The me in the mirror could never be the perfect Mommy I wanted to be. And I was tired, so tired, of trying to live up to all that the name implied.

Then one night, I read in my Bible about the day Jesus welcomed the little children into his arms.

(Matthew 19:13-15)

I pictured kids of all sizes and personalities clinging to Jesus' strong arms. And what struck me most was not what Jesus did in those three verses, but what He didn't do.

Jesus didn't require the children to prove their worth before they could climb on His knee. He didn't ask if they'd completed their to-do lists or washed their faces. He didn't interrogate their imperfections or analyze their accomplishments.

In fact, He didn't even ask their names. He simply welcomed them all because they were His.

And He does the same for us, dear moms. Whether we have children clinging to our knees or teens clustering around our tables, Jesus invites us to draw near to Him and know Him, to be lavished by His love and delighted by His mercy.

Not because we're perfect moms, but because we're His precious kids.

These devotions are a simple reminder of whose you are. They are an invitation to know Jesus more surely and to trust Him more deeply. They are tales from the trenches that will remind us that our greatest calling as moms isn't to live up to a name, but to point our children to the One whose name is above all names.

His name is Jesus and His lap has room for all of us.

- Alicia Bruxvoort

hey mama · *devotional*

week 1

identity

"Therefore, if anyone is in Christ, he is a new creation;
old things have passed away; behold, all things have become new."

2 Corinthians 5:17

Am I A Bad Mom?

By Lysa TerKeurst

"He says, 'Be still, and know that I am God'..." Psalm 46:10a (NIV)

Have you ever struggled with letting a circumstance define you? This seems to be a lesson God lets me live over and over again. He wants to be my only definition of who I am.

I am a child of God, holy and dearly loved.

I know this. I teach this. I believe this. Yet it is so easy for me to slip into redefining myself when situations arise.

Several years ago, one of my precious, precious, precious yet just-as-apt-to-sin-as-the-rest-of-us kids was called to the principal's office — on the very day I received an invitation to speak at a national parenting conference.

With my head I was able to see the situation for what it was: My child is in the process of being shaped. My child is strong, and while this will serve her well later in life, strength in an immature little person begs to be disciplined. She is a sweet child who made a not-so-sweet choice.

However, in my heart I felt like a failure. I wanted to decline the opportunity to speak and crawl into a hole. A part of me felt as though I'd personally been called to the principal's office, as the voice of condemnation started haunting me: You are a bad mom. You have a bad child. You have a bad home.

Quietly, I slipped away with Jesus and did what I'd done a hundred times before. I held those condemnations up to the Lord and asked Him to help me see this situation the way He wanted me to see it. Not the way others see it, not the way my heart is tempted to see it, but the way He sees it.

Matthew 7:24-27 brings some perspective: "Therefore everyone who hears these words of mine and puts them into practice is like a wise man who built his house on the rock. The rain came down, the streams rose, and the winds blew and beat against that house; yet it did not fall, because it had its foundation on the rock. But everyone who hears these words of mine and does not put them into practice is like a foolish man who built his house on sand. The rain came down, the streams rose, and the winds blew and beat against that house, and it fell with a great crash" (NIV).

Do you know what amazes me about these verses? Both the person doing right and the person doing wrong experienced hard times. In each case, the rains came, the streams rose and the wind blew and beat against the house.

Just because we're parents living out God's principles for life doesn't mean we won't face difficult circumstances.

God's Spirit spoke to my heart that day and said, "Let Me invade your natural flesh reaction. Instead of letting your mind run wild with this, sit with Me for a while. Be still, and know that I am God."

hey mama · *devotional*

Am I A Bad Mom?

By Lysa TerKeurst

So I sat and prayed. I went from defining myself as a failure of a mom to being a praying mom who can face hardships in a godly way. The frustration diffused as I determined to look at the situation from God's perspective.

God's truth reassured me. I am not a bad mom. My child is not a bad child. My home is not a bad home.

This situation is a call to action.

There is a character issue that needs to be addressed within the heart of my child. And kids are supposed to have character issues that need to be addressed. That's why God gave them parents. That's why God gave me this specific child. God sees within me the ability to be the one He's perfectly designed to raise this child.

When hard times come and beat against our stability, we must determine to hear God's words and put them into practice. Then nothing can topple our peace, security or true identity.

I'm not sure who else needed to hear that — but I know I did. So dry your tears, sweet mama. Today is a new day. A day when we will only be defined by God's truth and grace as we navigate this wild wonder called parenthood.

What was great today...

_____
_____

What was hard today...

_____
_____

A prayer for my children...

_____
_____

devotional · **hey mama**

Not the Same

By Lynn Cowell

"When the people of the land come before the LORD at the appointed feasts, whoever enters by the north gate to worship is to go out the south gate; and whoever enters by the south gate is to go out the north gate. No one is to return through the gate by which he entered, but each is to go out the opposite gate."
Ezekiel 46:9 (NIV 1984)

As soon as my eyes opened I knew it was going to be one of "those" days. I think that saying, "If mama ain't happy, ain't nobody happy" was created for days like this. I was sad, disappointed, frustrated and empty.

But I couldn't put my finger on why I felt all of these emotions. I just knew I had to get out of the house before everyone woke up and my feelings steered our day in the wrong direction.

I put on my tennis shoes and started out the front door. Though unsure of where I was going to run, I was certain of the length: far! Far enough for me to come back with a different perspective. What I needed was to get alone with Jesus, to have Him fill me, and exchange my negative emotions with His peace, truth and life.

As I started my run, old thoughts poured into my head. You are not beautiful. You are not special. Your life doesn't count. After years of reading, studying and even teaching the Truth, it was hard to believe I still struggled with these dark thoughts.

As lies poured in, I remember scriptures stored in my mind and heart. He sees me as beautiful. He says He is wild about me. He is more than enough for me. He is all I need.

Mulling over these precious promises from God's Word, tears began to pour. This is what I needed.

I didn't need more words of affirmation from my husband. I didn't need another pat on the back from a friend. I needed a new outpouring of love from my Love. I needed to be reminded of who He says I am, to give up the old lies and replace them with His Truths.

When we come into God's presence, He fills us. The Lord changes us so that we are not the same as we were when we came to Him. Ezekiel 46:9 represents this exchange of old for new. The people of Israel were told when they came into the temple area to worship, they were to enter through one gate and exit through the opposite gate.

So the same should be true with us; we are "not to go back as we came, but more holy, and heavenly, and spiritual" (Matthew Henry). As we enter into our special times with God, we need to come out the "opposite gate," different than the way we went in.

After an hour of running, crying and talking to God, I was not the same when I returned home. Now, I was ready. Ready to be the wife and mom my family needed. Restored into a vessel that God could use. Being with Jesus had changed me.

hey mama · devotional

Not the Same

By Lynn Cowell

What was great today...
_____
_____

What was hard today...
_____
_____

A prayer for my children...
_____
_____

devotional · **hey mama**

Overcoming the Doubts of Motherhood

By Tracie Miles

"Such confidence we have through Christ before God. Not that we are competent in ourselves to claim anything for ourselves, but our competence comes from God." 2 Corinthians 3:4-5 (NIV)

It was another one of those days when I wondered why God ever thought I was capable of being a mother.

I haven't always thought that way. When my children were younger, parenting seemed easier. I nursed their little wounds, played their favorite games, helped with homework and tucked them into bed each night with prayers and goodnight kisses.

But years passed and my sweet little ones started maturing, with their own opinions, hormones, friends, social lives and tempers. My heart broke with each disagreement. Frustration rose with every disrespectful word. My fears elevated, worry became my middle name, and at times, it seemed every ounce of patience had dripped out of my body.

So on that particular day, when it seemed I could do nothing right, insecurities and doubts flooded my mind.

With a heavy sigh, I slipped away to my room, sunk onto my bed, rested my head in my hands and prayed. I asked God for guidance, understanding and patience (lots of it). I prayed for the strength to continue standing strong in my parenting beliefs, even if they made me unpopular with my children and their friends. I prayed for peace and joy to fill my heart, even when our house didn't seem peaceful or joyful.

But then a confession slipped from my lips: "Lord, I obviously don't know how to be a parent now. I feel painfully inadequate and incapable of doing it right."

Through a quiet whisper to my spirit, the word "confidence" popped into my thoughts. God gently reminded me that depending on my own strength would eventually shake my confidence because deep down, I know my weaknesses.

Despite how hard I tried to be the mom God called me to be, I always fell short in my own eyes. Plus, I allowed difficult situations or comparison to other parents to shake my confidence. I needed to start depending on His strength to find my confidence instead.

Later that day, I searched for scriptures relating to "confidence" and came across today's key verses, which soothed this mama's heart. The Apostle Paul in 2 Corinthians reassures us that although life can cause us to doubt our capabilities, we can always find strength and confidence by trusting in the Lord.

When we rely on God in everything we do, including raising our children, we can be confident He will equip us for this calling of motherhood.

On those days when we doubt our strength, we can ask God for His strength to persevere.

On those days when we feel like the least-liked person in our homes, we can ask for confidence to stand strong in our beliefs.

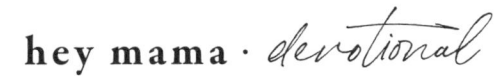

hey mama · *devotional*

Overcoming the Doubts of Motherhood

By Tracie Miles

On those days when we question whether or not we're cut out to be a parent, we can find assurance knowing God will surely stay beside us during the journey.

Most importantly, on those days when we find ourselves hiding in our bedrooms, we can boldly approach the throne of God, knowing with full confidence He hears our prayers and will give us wisdom to carry out this task of parenting.

That was not the last day I felt inadequate and insecure about my parenting skills. But now when those feelings creep in, I remember to pause and seek holy confidence.

The question we should ask ourselves when doubt creeps in isn't whether we're perfect parents. Instead, we can ask whether our children will look back and be thankful we loved them enough to pray and persevere through the hardest of days.

And that alone will be a rich reward.

What was great today…

_____

_____

What was hard today…

_____

_____

A prayer for my children…

_____

_____

devotional · **hey mama**

When You Wish You Were a Different Mommy

By Alicia Bruxvoort

"And *finally* He said to me, 'My grace is enough to cover and sustain you. My power is made perfect in weakness.' *So ask me about my thorn,* inquire about my weaknesses, and I will gladly go on and on — *I would rather stake my claim in these* and have the power of the Anointed One at home within me."
2 Corinthians 12:9 (The Voice)

When my firstborn was 3 years old, he told me he wished he had a different mommy.

He spat the words from the seat of his faded red time-out chair where he'd landed after digging holes in the neighbor's yard. He was certain that another mommy would understand that the best dinosaur bones were buried in the flowerbed across the street.

I'd remained silent, the angry words hanging between us like the strand of hair dangling over my son's icy blue eyes. But every piece of my wounded spirit had agreed with my fiery boy. I wish you had a different mommy, too, my heart cried.

Truth be told, I didn't want my son to exchange me for a new mommy; I just wished that I could be a different mommy. One who laughed more, forgave quicker and floundered less. One who never yelled in frustration or cried in exhaustion, and could turn scraps of paper into a Pinterest-worthy craft and bake a birthday cake from scratch. I wished I were a mom who innately knew how to parent children with temperaments unlike my own.

At first, I assumed my insecurities would disappear in time ... that once I figured out how to be a fabulous mom, my parenting flaws would fade. I read dozens of parenting books and studied the habits of moms who seemed to have it all together. But ironically, the more children I had, the more apparent my shortcomings became.

Ten years later as I sat exhausted, rocking our fitful fifth-born, I eyeballed the mess around me — laundry and Lego piles, homework folders and smelly gym bags — and exhaled a discouraged sigh. Then, in a moment of vulnerable honesty, I confessed my angst to my husband.

"I feel like I'm not enough. I can't ever do enough. Love enough. Work enough. Pray enough ..." Jostling the fussy infant in my arms, I felt that familiar churn of self-doubt rising in my stomach.

My husband stared at me, his tender gaze reflecting my pain. "You don't have to be enough," he murmured quietly. "That's Jesus' job."

I let his reassuring words seep deep into my splintered soul. In my striving to be enough, I'd forgotten that Christ's perfect plan for my children depends on His faithfulness, not my flawlessness.

Late that night, I opened my Bible to 2 Corinthians 12:9 and underlined this sacred pledge: "*My grace is enough to cover and sustain you. My power is made perfect in weakness.*" Then I wrote a simple declaration in the margin of my Bible: "I am not enough, but Jesus is."

hey mama · *devotional*

When You Wish You Were a Different Mommy

By Alicia Bruxvoort

From that moment on, I began to replace my fears with faith.

Instead of spending all of my energy on futile attempts to be a perfect mom, I chose to spend time getting to know my perfect Savior. I committed to reading God's Word daily and investing in prayer, memorizing Scripture and practicing the habit of gratitude. I "staked my claim" in the promises of Christ, and slowly, my qualms were quelled.

Today, I can humbly say that my firstborn's wish has come true. I am a different mommy. I'm still not enough for my children, but Jesus is. As I trust in His sufficiency and rest in His grace, I'm learning to live in His strength rather than obsess over my weaknesses. Because this far-from-perfect mommy has discovered a liberating truth — we have a Savior who is an expert at filling holes (eve dinosaur-sized ones).

What was great today…

_____

_____

What was hard today…

_____

_____

A prayer for my children…

_____

_____

devotional · **hey mama**

Embracing Who I Am

By Lysa TerKeurst

"But the angel said to her, 'Do not be afraid, Mary; you have found favor with God.'" Luke 1:30 (NIV)

Ten years ago, I sat in a seminar listening to a very organized mom talking about how she parented her kids. She was an amazing woman; a super mom in my eyes.

I held up my feeble efforts with my three toddlers and determined I stunk as a mother. I thought that maybe if I went home and imitated her, I could enter into the world of super moms.

I mentally listed out what I discerned must be her secret to success and set about to be just like her. But it didn't take me long to become absolutely miserable. I mentally beat myself up for not having what it obviously took to be a great mom. What was wrong with me?

I begged God to make me just like her — that really good mom. And then one day in Bible study, I read the story of Mary, the teenage mother of Jesus. My heart beat fast as I realized she didn't meet the standard of super mom I'd set for myself.

Somehow, just as she was, God chose her to be Jesus' mother. And the only qualification that she seemed to have was her willingness.

I made the choice to try and let go of all those expectations I had for myself as a mom. I let go of the comparisons to other moms. I laid down the measuring stick of perfection. And I simply bowed my head and gave God my willingness.

Slowly, I started to see my own unique qualities as a mom instead of always focusing on the places I felt I fell so short.

I may not be the most organized mom, but I'm a fun mom willing to drop my to-do list in the name of spontaneity.

I may not do sit-down devotions with my kids every morning, but I'm good at helping my kids see God working in situations all throughout our days.

I may not sew a lick, but I know where to find an alterationist that is the bomb.

I may not always keep my cool in the everyday aggravations of life, but throw something big at me and somehow I'll be the calmest person in the room.

Sure, I have a lot of room for growth in my mothering. God and I work on things daily. But over the past 10 years I've learned how to embrace who I am and the beauty of living fully as me.

And while I still fall short at times, I'm finally learning that being fully me is so much better than an imitation of someone else.

I have the exact qualities God knew my kids would need in a mother. So, each day, I hold up my willingness and ask God to make me the best version of me I can be.

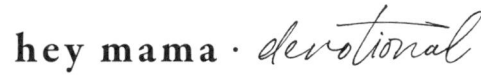

Embracing Who I Am

By Lysa TerKeurst

What was great today...
_____
_____

What was hard today...
_____
_____

A prayer for my children...
_____
_____

devotional · **hey mama**

When You Feel You're Not Enough

By Sharon Jaynes

"But he said to me, 'My grace is sufficient for you, for my power is made perfect in weakness.' Therefore I will boast all the more gladly about my weaknesses, so that Christ's power may rest on me."
2 Corinthians 12:9 (NIV)

As soon as my first-grade teacher held up that initial spelling flashcard, I knew I was in trouble.

Just 6 years old, I'd skipped off to school with a new box of crayons, a Swiss polka-dotted dress and fresh hope that I would be smart. But first grade only confirmed my greatest fear: I was "not enough."

We lined up our miniature wooden chairs in a row like a choo-choo train. The teacher held up a spelling flashcard for us to identify the word. If we missed the word, we had to go to the caboose. I spent most of the first grade in the caboose. I just couldn't spell. For some reason, I especially had trouble with the word "the."

I'll help her, my teacher must have thought. She made me a nametag that read t-h-e, and I had to wear it for two weeks. Students came up to me and asked, "Why are you wearing that tag?"

"Is your name 'The'?"

"What's wrong with you?"

Eventually, I learned how to spell "the", but that's not all I learned. I learned I wasn't as smart as everybody else, and once again, not enough. Although I ended up doing well in school, many times I've still felt like that little girl in the caboose.

Moses was also someone who felt he wasn't good enough. When God spoke through a burning bush and called Moses to lead His people out of Egyptian bondage, he had a big case of the "not-good-enoughs."

That's when he had a one-sided argument with God. Moses told God he was the wrong man for the job. He wasn't brave enough, strong enough, smart enough, eloquent enough, charismatic enough or confident enough.

At one point, Moses asked God, *"Suppose I go to the Israelites and say to them, 'The God of your fathers has sent me to you,' and they ask me, 'What is his name?' Then what shall I tell them?"*

And God replied to Moses, *"I AM WHO I AM. This is what you are to say to the Israelites: 'I AM has sent me to you'"* (Exodus 3:13-14, NIV).

Moses was 80 years old when he argued with God. But even the weakest knees in the hands of I AM can become a mighty force to be reckoned with.

I'll go out on a limb and say that you, too, have likely struggled with feelings of inferiority, insecurity and inadequacy. And the underlying statement feeding the sense of worthlessness is "I'm not _____ enough." You can fill in the blank with a number of qualities. False beliefs such as …

I'm not strong enough.

I'm not experienced enough.

When You Feel You're Not Enough

By Sharon Jaynes

I'm not talented enough.

I'm not brave enough.

I'm not pretty enough.

But here's what we need to remember: Whatever positive characteristic we feel we are not, God is.

Whatever we need, God is. He is the God who fills in our gaps; He is I AM who fills in our blanks. When we say, "I'm not strong enough," God says, "I AM."

When we say, "I'm not smart enough," God says, "I AM."

When we say, "I'm not good enough," God says, "I AM."

Once we let go of the lies that we're not enough ... and take hold of the truth that we're more than enough because of Jesus' presence and power in us ... then we'll be set free from paralyzing insecurity and on our way to experiencing courageous confidence to do everything He calls us to do. We'll get out of the caboose and sit up front with the engineer.

Want to know something amazing? One of my greatest weaknesses as a child was spelling words. And now that is what God has called me to do today ... write with words. I stand with Paul, who lamented about his weakness: *"But he [God] said to me, 'My grace is sufficient for you, for my power is made perfect in weakness.' Therefore I will boast all the more gladly about my weaknesses, so that Christ's power may rest on me"* (2 Corinthians 12:9).

That's what happens when we allow God to fill in our blanks. He turns what we perceive as our greatest weakness into our greatest strength.

What is God calling you to do today? Where do you feel you're not enough? Oh friend, because of Jesus' finished work on the cross, and His power in you, you are more than enough! Don't forget it.

What was great today...

What was hard today...

A prayer for my children...

devotional · **hey mama**

end of week 1

What did I learn about God this week?

_____
_____
_____
_____
_____
_____

How can I apply this to motherhood?

_____
_____
_____
_____
_____
_____

hey mama · *devotional*

week 2

overcoming
fear

"Cast all your anxieties on Him, for He cares for you."

1 Peter 5:7

"My grace is sufficient for you,
for my power is made perfect in weakness."

2 Corinthians 12:9a

~~I AM INADEQUATE~~

~~I AM INADEQUATE~~

~~I AM INADEQUATE~~

Calming My Heart

By Karen Ehman

"Then he went down with them and came to Nazareth and was obedient to them. His mother kept all these things in her heart. And Jesus increased in wisdom and stature, and in favor with God and with people." Luke 2:51-52 CSB

Neatly lined notebook paper. Sharpened number two pencils. A brand-new box of brightly colored crayons. A sturdy lunch box ready for the first PB&J of the year. Permission slips. Sports schedules. Class lists. So many details and so much stuff!

When it comes to back to school shopping, three-ring binders can seem almost like a three-ring circus. Gone are the lazy days of summer. The fall school routine brings new courses, loads of homework and many extra curricular activities.

While the arrival of the school year brings a fresh start — and soon the change of seasons — it can also bring a lot of worry to a mama's heart.

Our thoughts turn toward our children's interaction with others. We wonder how our timid child will fare in a brand-new classroom, when most of his friends are in another class. We fret about our prank-pulling middle schooler, earnestly hoping he doesn't make a habit of getting called to the principal's office. We fear for our high school student, worried she will start hanging around the wrong crowd.

Or we stress over academic concerns. Will our struggling first-grader ever make progress in her reading? Will math ever click with our fifth-grader who gets hives when she sees a story problem? Will our high schooler get into his hoped-for university?

Besides relational and academic matters, we also long for kids who are spiritually and physically healthy and strong. If left unchecked, our thoughts and concerns as mothers can wreak havoc on our hearts as we allow the tentacles of worry to choke out our joy.

We find an antidote to worry in the Gospel of Luke and the story of Mary and Jesus.

Luke 2 mentions four areas Jesus grew in as a young boy: *"And Jesus increased in wisdom and stature, and in favor with God and with people"* (Luke 2:52, CSB). Our Lord grew wiser each year. He physically grew. His relationship with His heavenly Father continually strengthened. Jesus even gained favor with people here on earth who saw Him day to day.

And how I love the simple sentence that precedes this: *"His mother kept all these things in her heart.* (Luke 2:51b, CSB).

When Mary was mothering Jesus, she tucked thoughts of her son safely in her heart. Some Bible translations say she "treasured" them. Others use the word "cherished." The original Greek word meant, "to keep safe or hold fast." In none of these descriptions do we see Mary fretting and fussing, worried and anxious, disquieted and unsettled. She pondered about her son and His growth, but she didn't allow her mama heart to become rattled.

hey mama · *devotional*

Calming My Heart

By Karen Ehman

Whatever season we're in, let's turn our anxious thoughts into treasured prayers, kept safe and held fast by our loving Father — the one who knows our hearts and loves our children even more than we do. When a concern pops up in our mind, let's drop to our knees and carry that concern to God. When we start to fear for our child's future, let's petition the only one who knows exactly what the future holds.

When we turn our worries into our prayers, we create space in our hearts to treasure and cherish the sweet moments with our kids. These paper-and-pencil school days won't last forever.

Let's delight in all that God is teaching our kids, whether it's how to read, how to forge friendships or how to solidify their walk with Him. And realize they aren't the only ones being taught; we moms are learning a life-long lesson in trusting and treasuring, knowing God is always in control.

What was great today...

_____

_____

What was hard today...

_____

_____

A prayer for my children...

_____

_____

devotional · **hey mama**

God Has No Grandchildren

By Brenda Bradford Ottinger

"... He would get up early in the morning and offer a burnt offering for each of them. For Job said to himself, 'Perhaps my children have sinned and have cursed God in their hearts.' This was Job's regular practice."
Job 1:5b (NLT)

Exactly one minute ago, my eldest son was learning to drive — according to Mom-Time, that is. Now here we are, cruising the backroads of Surreal-ville, as my third son has found his way behind a wheel. These are the moments when I sigh in solidarity with Dr. Seuss: How did it get so late so soon?

Oh, how far the Lord and I have come.

When I first started surrendering a driver to the roads, any notion of relaxation before my child returned was a fancy of futility. I longed for bygone days when I could see my children's faces in the rearview mirror as I drove them everywhere their sweet feet needed to go.

But once upon an ordinary Thursday while awaiting my son's return (in full-on anxious mom mode — and why didn't he text me when he got there, anyway?), the Lord interrupted my nerves, etching a tender truth on my peace-parched heart.

Sweet Daughter, His whisper cut through the noise, "it's not you who's been protecting them. From the swaddled womb to the steering wheel, all along it's been Me".

And in the newfound calm of that moment, tears and chains began to fall.

While I'd tried to control their safety with my worry (Lord, forgive me), He'd been holding their lives in His palm, giving His angels charge over these children of mine ... children of His.

That day, God granted wings to my worry-worn soul, shattering longstanding chains that bound my psyche to the lie that panic provides protection.

You see, I'd mistakenly tried to supplant God as watchman over my household. The more I labored, stressed and feared — in vain — to build a safe house for my people via the hollow frame of worry, the more frantic I became. My heart held fear so tightly that it couldn't grasp freedom. And in my frenzy, I overlooked the truth that these children of mine were born of His vision long before they were born of my body.

Dear friend, can you relate? Do you also struggle with fear clothed in protection's innocence?

Will she get a spot on the team? Will his heart be broken? Will she make a friend? Will another driver pull out in front of him? Will the diagnosis scar her? Will he accept Jesus as his Savior? Will she tune in to the heartbeat of God?

Whether it's a son or daughter, niece or nephew, neighbor or student — many are the cares of a nurturing heart.

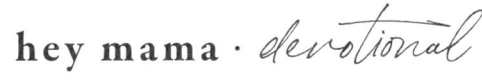

hey mama · *devotional*

God Has No Grandchildren

By Brenda Bradford Ottinger

Lately, I'm inspired by Job's approach to his concerns for his children, *"... He would get up early in the morning and offer a burnt offering for each of them. For Job said to himself, 'Perhaps my children have sinned and have cursed God in their hearts.' This was Job's regular practice"* (Job 1:5b). Job understood his greatest influence was in a posture of prayer. And I'm reminded that this, too, is my place of surrender.

Because the truth and the grace of it all is, our fear offers our loved ones exactly no amount of protection. Peace cannot be found in the sound of their tires pulling into the drive, in their making perfect choices or in the pseudo-control of my worries. Satisfaction never stays, for life is fluid, so there's always another fear to "worship."

The relief we crave seeps in as we surrender fear and control, trading them for prayer, freedom and the peace of knowing the children in our lives are the handiwork of their heavenly Father's heart.

God has no grandchildren — only children who've trusted Him as their Savior to guide and direct their lives. He alone knit them and knows them, and has kept them under His faithful watch since He set them down in our spheres of influence.

Oh, that our trust would make itself at home in faith, not fear: His power draws depths our anxiety can't access.

What was great today...

_____

_____

What was hard today...

_____

_____

A prayer for my children...

_____

_____

devotional · **hey mama**

God's Mighty Warrior

By Arlene Pellicane

"When the angel of the LORD appeared to Gideon, he said, 'The LORD is with you, mighty warrior.'" Judges 6:12 (NIV)

I remember being a new mom and finding great solace in the bathroom. Some days I wanted to hide in there for long stretches of time from my energetic toddler. My son Ethan loved to turn off the light in the bathroom and shut the door. He would giggle from the other side.

I didn't care about being in the dark. I was just happy to be left alone for a moment. I didn't feel at all like a mighty warrior. I felt more like a nobody hiding out.

This is how I imagine Gideon's disposition was in Judges 6. During this time, the Midianites had overpowered and dominated Israel for seven years. The Israelites hid out in mountains, caves and forts. Like an invasion of locusts, the enemy came in and took over. They destroyed Israel's crops and devastated the country. In desperation, the people of Israel cried out to God for help.

Perhaps something has overwhelmed you in your life. Maybe you relate to Gideon's situation like this …

The crying children overpowered the mothers. Because of their whiny, unhappy little ones, the mothers made hideouts wherever they could find them — the bathroom, local coffee shop or hidden in the laundry room. The children wreaked havoc in the kitchen and family room. Their toys were like an invasion of locusts. The mothers, reduced to wearing sweats and cutting up food all day, cried out to God for help.

We can all take heart, because in the midst of Gideon's hopelessness, God shows up in a big way. While Gideon was hiding in a winepress, threshing wheat, the angel of the Lord appears. This was not just any angel. This is understood to be an Old Testament appearance of God Himself declaring:

"The LORD is with you, mighty warrior" (Judges 6:12b).

"Go in the strength you have and save Israel out of Midian's hand. Am I not sending you?" (Judges 6:14b, NIV)

Gideon may have looked behind him to see if the angel of the Lord was addressing someone else. After all, he was hardly qualified to save Israel, coming from the weakest clan in Manasseh and being the least in his family (verse 15). Yet apparently to God, Gideon was a mighty warrior.

I believe God sees mighty warriors in each of us too. Imagine going about your daily work, making dinner, paying bills or sorting laundry and God appears to you saying, "The LORD is with you, mighty warrior." This would undoubtedly change your life.

It doesn't matter how you were raised as a child, whether you're rich or poor, God makes victors out of the ordinary and overlooked. God seems to delight in working powerfully through unexpected "warriors" such as Gideon, Rahab and Ruth. Don't let your past determine your present or your circumstances dictate your worth. God is the giver of new life.

hey mama · devotional

God's Mighty Warrior

By Arlene Pellicane

Notice God appeared to Gideon in private. Wheat was normally threshed in open spaces, typically on a hilltop so the breeze could blow away the chaff. But fearful of the Midianites, Gideon worked hidden away in a sunken winepress.

God can meet you in the privacy of your home when you're tending to your family members, thinking no one notices your efforts. You might be caring for a toddler, teenager or aging parent. Or you may be at your job, doing your daily work when God shows up to speak to you. Gideon was a simple man living a normal life, but as he fulfilled his everyday duties, God showed up to do the miraculous.

Gideon was teachable because he listened to what the angel of the Lord said. He rose to the daunting occasion of delivering the Israelites. He didn't do it perfectly, but God's strength is perfected in weakness, isn't it?

So when you look in the bathroom mirror today, what will you see? Even if you're hiding in there, you can choose to see a mighty warrior for God.

What was great today...

_____

_____

What was hard today...

_____

_____

A prayer for my children...

_____

_____

devotional · **hey mama**

What if the Next Big Step God Wants You to Take is Small?

By Lysa TerKeurst

"Listen for GOD'S voice in everything you do, everywhere you go; he's the one who will keep you on track." Proverbs 3:6 (MSG)

It was a hot day inside and outside at the orphan village in Liberia. The 12 boys inside, practicing their choir music, found their eyes wandering over to the soccer field, where the promise of fun and the cheers of their friends tugged at them.

They were feeling the pull of wanting to go outside and play soccer. But these boys determined the choir was worth the sacrifice.

Years earlier, Liberia had been ravaged by a civil war that left more than 25,000 orphans to be cared for. So to raise money and support, an a cappella boys' choir was formed to travel throughout the country of Liberia and perform in churches.

Two of the teenage boys in that choir, Jackson and Mark, had been orphaned as babies when their parents and most of their siblings were killed by rebel forces.

Night after night, these boys knelt beside their makeshift beds and poured out prayers of thanksgiving and hope that one day they'd hear six simple yet life-changing words, "You are my child — welcome home."

God had a perfect design for their prayers to be answered and worked miracle after miracle to bring the boys' choir to America. But little did I know our family would be part of the answer to Mark and Jackson's prayers.

Our life was busy and full, and we were enjoying being the parents of three little girls. So you can imagine my surprise the night I went to see The Liberian Boys' Choir concert at our church that I was stirred to consider adoption.

As I sat in the concert, God whispered to my heart that two of those boys singing were mine. No, I thought. Not me.

I felt like sticking my fingers in my ears and singing, La, la, la, la, la ... I'm not listening to You, God! But the stirring in my heart wouldn't stop.

I decided to try a new tactic with Him. Lord, I just came here tonight to bring my girls to a simple little cultural event. I'm not looking for a major life change. Our life is already very full with work, speaking, writing and homeschooling three girls. Besides, all my friends would think I was crazy.

But God wasn't discouraged by my response. His directive in my heart became more intense as the evening went on. After the concert, I asked the coordinator of the event which of the boys still needed homes. He told me that eight of the boys still needed to find families and encouraged me to walk into the reception area where they were. If God intended for some of these boys to be ours, he was sure I'd know it.

Reluctantly, I walked into the reception area. In a matter of seconds, Jackson and Mark walked up to me, wrapped their arms around me, and called me Mom.

What if the Next Big Step God Wants You to Take is Small?

By Lysa TerKeurst

I was moved and terrified at the same time.

What began as a small heart prompting had turned into a very big decision for our family.

After talking about it, we cried out to God desperate for His guidance and wisdom. We pondered every aspect and wrestled with this decision deep in our spirits.

Still, doubts and questions flooded our minds: How could we financially increase the size of our family?

How would we find the time in our already crammed schedule? How would we raise boys? How would we find room in our home? The list went on and on.

One day, I called a friend and poured out my heart. I told her I could list many other parents who were much more qualified to adopt. She patiently listened without much response as I asked, "Why me?"

Then quietly and prayerfully she answered: "Because God knew you'd say yes, Lysa."

I was stunned. It was the highest compliment I'd ever received. My heart was filled with joy as memories filled my mind of the years of small steps God had me take to reach the place where I could be prepared to take this much bigger step.

Now, over 10 years later, I think back to sitting in that church pew, just going about my ordinary life when God's extraordinary invitation burst forth. I could have so easily walked out of that church and ignored God's stirring. I've done that more times than I'd like to admit. But look at everything we would have missed out on, had I done that.

Hear my heart: I'm not saying everyone is called to adopt. Honestly, the next big step God wants you to take might actually be small. But we'll never know what that next step is if we don't "listen for GOD'S voice in everything we do, everywhere we go" as Proverbs 3:6 instructs us.

Each day we can look for His invitation to leave our plans behind to join Him in His wondrous work through small steps of obedience.

What was great today...

What was hard today...

A prayer for my children...

---

devotional · **hey mama**

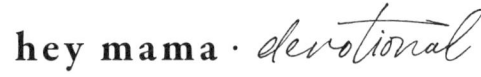

Where Your Tears Go

By Tracie Miles

"You keep track of all my sorrows. You have collected all my tears in your bottle. You have recorded each one in your book." Psalm 56:8 (NLT)

If there is one thing I'm known for, it's crying.

When one of my little ones scraped their knee, didn't make the sports team or were hurt by a friend's harsh words … I cried.

The first time my 16-year-old daughter pulled out of the driveway with her new license, when a boy broke her heart, and as she strolled across the stage last year in her blue graduation gown, I cried.

So when it came time to move her into her dorm room a couple months later, I feared my tears might be uncontrollable.

Although I was proud she was going to college, and it was time for her to spread her wings, the thought of her leaving seemed unbearable. The idea of not seeing her sweet smile every day, coupled with concern over her well-being, made my heart heavy.

I had a flashback of tears shed many years ago as my little girl, dressed in her tiny denim skirt and purple butterfly shirt, stood waving goodbye from the door of her kindergarten room. As I turned to leave my daughter in her dorm room, my waterworks started.

There were tears of happiness, gratitude and excitement. Tears of sadness, anxiety and motherly worry.

A part of me wondered if I should be crying in this situation. Many mothers would be thrilled to be dropping a child off at college. Was I being selfish with my tears?

In that moment of mixed emotions, I desperately needed God's comfort and reassurance, and I found it in Psalm 56:8.

In Psalm 56:8, God reminds us He is intimately concerned with every aspect of our lives. God doesn't judge whether our sorrow is "valid." But because of His compassion, He catches every tear that is shed. It doesn't matter how big or small, trivial or important, the sorrow might be.

In this Psalm, David expressed grief over his situation, which was truly dangerous. Saul wanted his own son to be king of Israel and was hunting David in order to murder him.

This forced David to constantly be on the move as he tried to escape. David was grieved, fearful and unsure about the future. Apparently tears flowed as he poured out his feelings to God. *"You keep track of all my sorrows. You have collected all my tears in your bottle. You have recorded each one in your book"* (Psalm 56:8).

hey mama · *devotional*

Where Your Tears Go

By Tracie Miles

David drew comfort in knowing that no matter what he was going through, God had great compassion on him and gathered all his precious tears in a bottle. David trusted God with his life and his future. He wasn't embarrassed about his tears, and we need not be either, even when we wish we could hold them back.

Life challenges us. Children grow. Seasons of change bump into our normal status quo. When this happens, tears often spring up, and efforts to contain them fall short.

Dropping your child off at kindergarten, college or any grade in between can evoke a variety of anxieties and emotions. As back-to-school season approaches, let's remember God has compassion on us and our children.

He is present with every tear shed, and we can count on Him to collect them. No matter what sorrow we face today, we can have confidence God cares.

What was great today...

_____

_____

What was hard today...

_____

_____

A prayer for my children...

_____

_____

devotional · **hey mama**

Changing History Through Prayer

By Sharon Glasgow

"In her deep anguish Hannah prayed to the LORD, weeping bitterly. And she made a vow, saying, 'LORD Almighty, if you will only look on your servant's misery and remember me, and not forget your servant but give her a son, then I will give him to the LORD for all the days of his life …" 1 Samuel 1:10-11a (NIV)

Hours before I was conceived, my mom got on her knees. "Lord, if You will give me a baby tonight I will dedicate it to You and for Your service all the days of its life. Amen." God answered her prayer that night, and all my days have been devoted to Him in large part due to the fervent prayers of my mom.

My mom followed in the footsteps of millions of mothers who prayed for their children. From the time of Samuel until this very day, some of our most influential Christian heroes became history makers because of their mothers' prayers.

Samuel's mother Hannah poured out her soul to the Lord for years, pleading for a son. Eventually, God granted her prayer requests with her son Samuel, who Hannah dedicated to the Lord (1 Samuel 1:10-11a). He grew in wisdom, became a great prophet and judge, and led the Israelites into victory over the mighty Philistines.

Susanna Wesley raised her sons, John (one of the greatest evangelists of the 1700s, speaking to crowds of more than 20,000) and Charles (who wrote over 9,000 hymns still sung today) in a home dedicated to the Word of God and prayer. In the midst of raising 10 children, she would spend two hours a day in personal prayer. On days she couldn't find a place of solitude, she would lift her apron over her head to be alone with God.

George Washington was known for his humility, perseverance and dignity. His mother Mary raised him and his siblings as a single mother after her husband died when George was 10. It is recorded that she went to a nearby rock outside her house to pray continually. George wrote letters to his mother while on the battlefield of the Revolutionary War, that he escaped death when bullets went through his coat and horses were shot out from under him. Miracle after miracle happened to George, and he honored his praying mother with these words: "All that I am I owe to my mother."

Billy Graham has led nearly three million people to freedom in Christ and has preached the gospel to more than 80 million people during his lifetime. He has said of all the people he has ever known, his mother, Morrow, had the greatest influence on his life. She would gather the family to listen to the Bible and pray together. She and his dad would pray for Billy each morning at 10.

Every Christian mother contending, interceding and praying for her children has the potential to change the course of history for God's glory. Our world is in need of God-filled history makers to rise up. I'm going to pray more diligently than ever for our children and their future and will stand on these promises of God:

Matthew 21:22, "And whatever things you ask in prayer, believing, you will receive" (NKJV).

hey mama · *devotional*

Changing History Through Prayer

By Sharon Glasgow

John 14:13-14, "And whatever you ask in My name, that I will do, that the Father may be glorified in the Son. If you ask anything in My name, I will do it" (NKJV).

I will pray as my mother, Hannah, Susanna, Mary and Morrow did for their children. I will pray for my children and for generations to come with unwavering passion and persistence. Will you join me?

Let's rise up and be strong in the Lord and in the power of His might as we pray to Him who is able to do immeasurably more than we can think or imagine.

What was great today...
_____
_____

What was hard today...
_____
_____

A prayer for my children...
_____
_____

devotional · **hey mama**

end of week 2

What did I learn about God this week?

How can I apply this to motherhood?

week 3

perspective

"Because of the Lord's great love we are not consumed,
for his compassions never fail. They are new every morning;
great is your faithfulness."

Lamentations 3:22-23

~~I HAVE TO BE PERFECT~~

"God made him who had no sin to be sin for us, so that in him we might become the righteousness of God."

2 Corinthians 5:21

Dreaming Amidst the Shattered Glass

By Meredith Houston Carr

"Now to him who is able to do immeasurably more than all we ask or imagine, according to his power that is at work within us, to him be the glory in the church and in Christ Jesus throughout all generations, for ever and ever! Amen." Ephesians 3:20-21 (NIV)

It had been a particularly exhausting day. My special needs son was driving me a special kind of crazy. My daughters couldn't share a single toy without erupting into ear-piercing shrieks. The to-do list multiplied. So in an effort to preserve my unraveling sanity and restore order, I called a time-out for each child.

But my son didn't see this time-out as a good thing. Emotion overwhelmed him, and he struggled to regulate the storm in his unique, autistic mind. In a flash, he grabbed a framed baby picture and hurled it onto the bathroom floor. Hard tile met fragile glass in a clash with no winner — only hundreds of jagged shards.

After ensuring his safety and cleaning up the mess, I stared at that picture. Shattered glass lay in random bits and pieces across the image of my husband and me, gazing at our son's newborn perfection.

Hot tears bubbled up and spilled over, with liquid pain pouring down my face. This broken picture symbolized a deeper brokenness permeating my heart, for glass wasn't the only thing to shatter in that moment. My dreams of what it would be like to mother this sweet boy shattered, too.

The new mom in that picture never imagined autism becoming a part of her story.

In agony, I cried out to my heavenly Father, and in His unceasing kindness, He brought to mind today's key verse:

"Now to him who is able to do immeasurably more than all we ask or imagine, according to his power that is at work within us, to him be glory in the church and in Christ Jesus throughout all generations, for ever and ever! Amen" (Ephesians 3:20-21).

Those words, "immeasurably more," pierced my aching heart. I was gently convicted of the small box I'd put God into — how I'd inadvertently transferred my own narrow vision of motherhood to Him.

In my pain, God opened my eyes to the reality that His plans reach far beyond what my fallible eyes can see. He overwhelmed my heart with love for moms and dads who, like me, face shattered dreams of their own. He infused me with hope that perhaps my pain could be the very thing that draws me into a deeper, sweeter fellowship with Him and with others facing a similar heartache.

And He graciously reminded me that even when I'm staring down circumstances that likely will not change, He can always change me. His joy and hope stand freely available, even as I tiptoe along the broken path.

When our dreams fall apart, it's hard to imagine something better is possible. But the truth in today's key verse gives us a powerful promise we can cling to in the face of disintegrating plans.

Dreaming Amidst the Shattered Glass

By Meredith Houston Carr

Shattered dreams are no reason to stop dreaming. Because of His great power at work within us, we can keep on dreaming. For where we see brokenness, God sees "immeasurably more" than even our wildest dreams!

Dear one, God is bigger than your greatest heartache and most shattering disappointment. He is undoubtedly good — even when your path is littered with broken glass. Broken glass is not the end of your story. Indeed, it may very well be the beginning.

Today, may we humbly, and with hearts full of hope, bring God our broken pieces. And may we trust Him enough to keep on dreaming.

What was great today...

_____
_____

What was hard today...

_____
_____

A prayer for my children...

_____
_____

devotional · **hey mama**

Planning Funerals That Won't Happen Today

By Lysa TerKeurst

"My frame was not hidden from you when I was made in the secret place, when I was woven together in the depths of the earth. Your eyes saw my unformed body; all the days ordained for me were written in your book before one of them came to be." Psalm 139:15-16 (NIV)

Several years ago, my then-teenage son came to me and asked if he could take his brother and sisters to go get ice cream. How fun! How thoughtful! "Sure," I said, "Let me grab my keys and we'll go."

"No, Mom — we sort of want to go just us kids," he quickly replied.

"Oh," and that's about all I could get my mouth to say as my brain started racing and reeling. In my mind, pictures started flashing of a terrible accident, a phone call from the police, planning a funeral and then thinking back to this moment when I could have said No.

And it was that strange sense that everything depended on me and my decisions that made me want to say: No. Absolutely not. You will stay home today. You will all stay home forever. I have to keep you safe.

Most of us moms live with this gnawing, aching, terrifying fear that something will happen to one of our children. We carry the pressure that ultimately everything rises and falls on whether or not we can control things. And mentally, too often we plan funerals that won't happen today.

We do it because we know the realities of living in a broken world where car accidents happen. Tragedy strikes old and young alike. We have no guarantees for tomorrow. And that's really hard on a mama's heart. When I was a teenager, I lost my baby sister in a tragic way — so I know devastating realities can happen.

If you've lost someone you love, I wish I could reach through this screen, squeeze your hand and whisper, "I'm so sorry. I understand. It's such a deep, deep pain." And a pain that we fear happening again.

That's where I was as I stood at the front window of my house fretting and watching as the entire contents of my mama heart piled into one car.

And I realized I had a choice.

I could run myself ragged creating a false sense of control that can't really protect them. Or, I could ask God to help me make wise decisions and choose to park my mind on the truth, which is:

God has assigned each of my kids a certain number of days.

My choices can add to the quality of their life, but not the quantity. They could be at home tucked underneath my wings, and if it's their day to go be with Jesus, they will go.

Our key verse confirms this: "My frame was not hidden from you when I was made in the secret place, when I was woven together in the depths of the earth. Your eyes saw my unformed body; all the days ordained for me were written in your book before one of them came to be" (Psalm 139:15-16).

Jesus conquered death so we don't have to be afraid of it any longer.

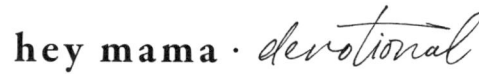

Planning Funerals That Won't Happen Today

By Lysa TerKeurst

Of course, the death of anyone I love would make me devastatingly sad, heartbroken and absolutely dazed with grief. But I don't have to be held captive by the fear of death.

"Since the children have flesh and blood, he [Jesus] too shared in their humanity so that by his death he might break the power of him who holds the power of death — that is, the devil — and free those who all their lives were held in slavery by their fear of death" (Hebrews 2:14-15, NIV).

Death is only a temporary separation. We will be reunited again.

In 2 Samuel 12, when David's infant child died, he confidently said, "I shall go to him, but he shall not return to me" (v. 23b, KJV). David knew he would see his child again — not just a faceless soul without an identity, but this child for whom he was longing. He would know him, hold him and kiss him. The separation death caused would be over.

I know these are heavy things to process. And I certainly don't claim that these truths will help you never, ever fear again. But I do hope these truths will settle your heart into a better place. A place where your heart is consumed with truth instead of fear.

What was great today…

_____

_____

What was hard today…

_____

_____

A prayer for my children…

_____

_____

devotional · **hey mama**

I Am Not Alone

By Whitney Capps

"Two people are better off than one, for they can help each other succeed. If one person falls, the other can reach out and help. But someone who falls alone is in real trouble." Ecclesiastes 4:9-10 (NLT)

I sat at my computer and typed, deleted and then re-typed the same email at least three times. Did I sound too desperate, too needy? Surely things weren't this bad. Maybe I just needed a little perspective. So I stopped and looked around.

Toys of a million varieties, parts and pieces were scattered across the floor. My 3-year-old and 2-year-old were still in their pajamas. It was nearly 10:30 a.m. and they'd been watching television far longer than any good mother should allow.

To top it off, my newborn was crying. I'd stuck him in the swing because I just needed a break. I hadn't showered in two days. At least I think it had been two days. I was in a time warp, so who could be sure? I knew I hadn't changed clothes in as many days. My t-shirt and sweatpants were stained with unmentionables.

Who was I kidding? Things really were this bad.

I turned back to the computer and typed an honest assessment of the situation. I hit send before my pride vetoed my cry for help. I wasn't going to pretend anymore. I needed to know I wasn't alone.

If I didn't send an SOS, things would go from bad to worse. So I did what scripture tells us to do in Ecclesiastes 4:9-10 ("Two people are better off than one, for they can help each other succeed. If one person falls, the other can reach out and help. But someone who falls alone is in real trouble") and called out to friends to help me out of this messy, sticky, stinky mess.

Girlfriends, I am struggling. Life with three boys under four is hard. Ryder is such an easy baby that I feel guilty voicing my weariness. And Cooper and Dylan are just little boys. I don't expect anything to be other than what it is right now. It's just that right now is rather taxing. I know every stage of motherhood is.

My life is no more difficult than yours. That's why I have started and stopped this email three times. I feel self-indulgent to talk about how parched my soul is. But I'm drowning in diapers, potty-training and milk.

In a matter of minutes my inbox filled with messages. I had asked my girlfriends to pray for me and pick me up from this pit. These amazing women came through in a big way, sharing some of the funniest stories I've ever heard and offering the kindest commiseration a new mom could want. I felt connected, accepted and loved.

Hearing their words in my head, I changed diapers, wiped noses and unloaded the dishwasher repeating:

I am not alone.

God's grace is sufficient.

Do the next thing.

hey mama · *devotional*

I Am Not Alone

By Whitney Capps

Why hadn't I asked for help sooner? What was I afraid of?

I knew what it was. I didn't want them to think less of me. Would they see the real me, and still love me?

My pride shouted, but my heart trembled.

In the moments before I sent that email I felt utterly alone. In the days that followed, I realized the fellowship I had gained was totally worth the embarrassment of admitting my fears and failures. As it turned out, these dear women didn't love me less for sharing; they loved me more.

Through their kind words, my friends did the best thing possible: They lifted my focus from myself and put it on Jesus. I learned not to depend on my own abilities, but to depend on Him.

Interestingly, I didn't have more confidence as a mom after that day. And I didn't suddenly get to take a shower every day. I realized I am absolutely inadequate. I am sincerely overwhelmed. But my friends reminded me that I'm not alone and my situation isn't unique to me.

As my friends promised to walk this journey with me, I discovered there's safety in numbers. In the quiet of my head and heart, sometimes the voice of fear and condemnation drowns out God's truth. With a resounding chorus, these girlfriends shouted truth so loudly it couldn't be ignored. It was just what I needed.

And they didn't care that I hadn't brushed my teeth.

What was great today...

What was hard today...

A prayer for my children...

---

devotional · **hey mama**

When Strong Moms Feel Quite Weak

By Lysa TerKeurst

"Have I not commanded you? Be strong and courageous. Do not be afraid; do not be discouraged, for the LORD your God will be with you wherever you go." Joshua 1:9 (NIV)

I stood at the vending machine infuriated.

More than annoyed. More than angry. More than mad.

Infuriated.

A girl can sometimes have an out-of-proportion response to the wrong she is experiencing. And like a compass pointing true north, this infuriation pointed somewhere. Somewhere I didn't want to explore.

I wanted a Diet Coke. So, I did what was necessary. I followed the rules. I put in the required money. I pushed the right button.

Only what I got wasn't at all what I wanted.

Something had gone wrong.

I clenched my fists and bit my lip.

And I knew. My out-of-proportion response wasn't really about a soda. It was about being disillusioned by one of my kids.

It was about my feeling that if I did all the right things, I would get all the right results. You do what's expected of you, and you'll get what you expect. Right?

Put in the money. Push the button. Get the Diet Coke.

Put in all the time and love. Intentionality. Prayer. Discipline. Bible lessons. Church. Dinners at the table. Talks at bedtime. Kisses. Hugs. Chores.

Push the button. Get the child who walks the straight and narrow.

But, no. Sometimes you get the unexpected.

And you know what I'm tempted to do as a mom? Draw a straight line from my child's wrong choice to my weakness in mothering.

That will just about kill a mama. It will crack her heart open and fill it with paralyzing regret of the past and fear for the future. And that's exactly where Satan wants us mamas to stay. Paralyzed.

But what if that's the wrong line to draw?

What if I'm supposed to draw a straight line from my child's wrong choice to my strength in mothering?

What if God said …

"What mom will rely on Me to make her strong enough, persevering enough, tough enough to bend without breaking under the weight of the choices this child will make?

When Strong Moms Feel Quite Weak

By Lysa TerKeurst

"What mom is willing to be humbled to the point of humiliation, yet not blinded to the wisdom to be discovered in this situation, much like finding diamonds hidden in deep places?

"What mom will not just pray for this child, but will truly pray this child all the way through their stuff?

"What mom will be courageous enough to let Me write her child's story?"

And then God points.

I can't say I ever wanted God to point in my direction. I can't. But sometimes we get the unexpected.

And I guess I'm just wanting to breathe hope into someone else's paralyzed place.

In Joshua 1:9, God clearly instructs us to remember the importance of staying strong when going into battle. In fact, He commands us to be! "Have I not commanded you? Be strong and courageous. Do not be afraid; do not be discouraged, for the LORD your God will be with you wherever you go."

Mama, you are strong. Persevering. Tough. Able to bend without breaking. Willing to be humbled to the point of humiliation. Not blinded. A hunter for wisdom. A praying-through-it woman. A courageous mama. One who wants her child to not just follow the rules, but follow God Himself.

Let me take your hand. And stand with you.

From that cracked open-heart place, a God-breathed strength will rise. Rise. Rise.

And help you declare to Satan, "You picked the wrong mama to mess with this time."

What was great today...

_____
_____

What was hard today...

_____
_____

A prayer for my children...

_____
_____

devotional · **hey mama**

Keeping Perspective
By Glynnis Whitwer

"Remember that you were slaves in Egypt and that the LORD your God brought you out of there with a mighty hand and an outstretched arm." Deuteronomy 5:15 (NIV 1984)

My little sister and I were an unstoppable team in the board game Pictionary. Within seconds we guessed each other's drawings, annoying our opponents in the process. Sometimes it was an unspoken memory shared by the two of us. Most often it was because we understood the concept of perspective.

For example, if we were attempting to draw a basketball, we immediately drew something else to create perspective. Otherwise, our teammates would waste time guessing that it was the sun, the earth or a face. A stick person holding the circle narrowed the guesses, because seeing objects in relation to each other helped reveal the truth.

Perspective made all the difference in the game, and it makes all the difference in how we handle life. Without perspective, small problems seem insurmountable, and we ignore warning signs. But with perspective, hard situations don't overwhelm, and we can find our way to thankfulness instead of despair.

To help me take a balanced approach to life's difficult times, I've developed a few perspective points. These points are hard-earned lessons in my life. By making them perspective points, I choose to find value in what would otherwise be dismal experiences. Now, when I'm faced with bad news, disappointment or failure, I grasp one of these perspective points, and like a compass pointing north, I can accurately assess the situation, and choose to be thankful.

One of the most difficult perspective points in my life is the death of my niece Christa in a car accident. In fact, at times I feel my life is divided in two parts: before and after Christa's death. With five children of my own, this devastating loss to our family has given me perspective on the challenges we face.

When one of my children makes a heart-breaking choice, I grieve and administer consequences. Then very quickly, like that magnetic force in a compass, perspective points me to thankfulness. Thank You Lord my son (or daughter) is alive.

Another perspective point is the economic downfall of the past few years. Finances have eased a bit, but we'll be battling our way out of that slump for years to come. Instead of being resentful, I find myself thankful for having money to spend at all. Thank You Lord for getting us through that rough time and for what I have to spend today.

In Deuteronomy 5:15 Moses gave the Israelites God's Ten Commandments. As Moses related "Observe the Sabbath day," he challenged the people with this sentence: "Remember that you were slaves in Egypt and that the LORD your God brought you out of there with a mighty hand and an outstretched arm." God was establishing a day of rest, but also a day to keep perspective and be thankful. He wanted people to remember the hard times so they could appreciate the good times even more.

hey mama · *devotional*

Keeping Perspective

By Glynnis Whitwer

Perspective points are arrows to thankfulness. They remind me God was faithful then and He will be faithful now. They remind me God was greater than my circumstances then, and still is today. Most importantly, they help me cultivate a thankful heart for what I have. The truth is, as long as we have breath, there is reason to be thankful and hopeful.

Let's identify perspective points in our lives. It's how we can find value in what seems a waste. They prove God can use anything for good, and help turn our hearts to gratitude instead of grumbling.

What was great today…

_____

_____

What was hard today…

_____

_____

A prayer for my children…

_____

_____

end of week 3

What did I learn about God this week?

_____
_____
_____
_____
_____
_____

How can I apply this to motherhood?

_____
_____
_____
_____
_____
_____

week 4

letting *go*

"Now the Lord is the Spirit, and where the Spirit of the Lord is, there is freedom."

2 Corinthians 3:17

~~I CAN'T DO THIS~~

"I can do all things through him who strengthens me."

Philippians 4:13

Freedom From the Facade

By Amy Carroll

"Be perfect, therefore, as your heavenly Father is perfect." Matthew 5:48 (NIV)

There's nothing like a picture from high school to remind you of your former goofy self. An old friend recently posted a picture of a group of us on a field trip that made me both giggle and blush.

There I stood in the middle of the Smithsonian Museum, posed in a feisty Charlie's Angels stance with my friends, big hair poofing and hip cocked like I owned the world. Remember that weird teen stage that was a mix of self-consciousness and arrogance?

I laughed at the picture, and then I started to think about that girl — the Amy of decades ago.

That opinionated girl who thought she understood the world — who had equal measures of sass, attitude and idealism — who always saw the best in people — who loved to be known as "a little different." That girl has turned into a woman who now feels comfortable in her own skin, but she disappeared behind a facade of her own making — a mask of perfection — for years in between.

I'm not sure when the change happened. Maybe it was when I tried to measure up in a legalistic church. Or maybe it was when I took on the weight of wanting to be the perfect wife and mom. But probably it was when I started valuing what others thought about me more than protecting the woman God had created me to be.

Day by day, the true me started to disappear. One small choice after another led me down a path of hiding behind a facade of perfection rather than living the full and free life God had for me. Maybe you recognize yourself here too. You've started creating a false

"I've-got-it-all-together" image to keep people from knowing the real you with your flaws and failures. It feels safer behind that wall, but it's exhausting. And it's soul-crushing.

For a while, even Scripture confused me on this matter, so I sought out a trusted friend to help me.

Across the table, I exclaimed to her, "But the Bible does tell us to be perfect! Right there in Matthew 5:48 Jesus says, 'Be perfect, therefore, as your heavenly Father is perfect.'" She just smiled and sent me home to do some studying and to look up the meaning of the word perfect in its context. I hurried home to do my assignment.

As the root definition of the word flashed onto my computer screen, I sat in teary-eyed silence. The truer translation of the word perfect in this verse is to be "whole," "complete" or "mature." The Amplified Bible says it this way, "You, therefore, will be perfect [growing into spiritual maturity both in mind and character, actively integrating godly values into your daily life], as your heavenly Father is perfect."

I might be mixed up about lots of things, but suddenly I had clarity on a big step toward breaking up with perfect. God is calling us from the hollowness of self-made perfection to the wholeness of God-given completion. He is doing a perfecting work in us, freeing us day by day from our false image of perfection, until we live in the freedom, joy and fullness of life for which we were made.

hey mama · *devotional*

Freedom From the Facade

By Amy Carroll

While our pursuit of perfection and a flawless image drains us of energy, God's work of perfecting fills us with peace. We can trust that God is big enough to turn even our flaws into something usable and to redeem the failures of our past. Living in God's image the beautiful unique women He created us to be, is a huge step toward true maturity.

Creating an image is measuring up. Living in God's image is filling up. Let's step into His image and complete our own!

What was great today…

_____

_____

What was hard today…

_____

_____

A prayer for my children…

_____

_____

devotional · **hey mama**

Why Every Mom Needs a Bouquet of Dead Flowers

By Alicia Bruxvoort

"We know what true love looks like because of Jesus. He gave His life for us, and He calls us to give our lives for our brothers and sisters." 1 John 3:16 (VOICE)

I'll never forget the Mother's Day my firstborn gave me a bouquet of dead daisies.

The evening before, I'd watched from the kitchen window as my son roamed the overgrown field in our backyard and proudly picked a handful of golden blooms. He'd sniffed the silky petals with an appreciative nod, then he'd marched inside and asked me for a shoebox, some tape and a roll of aluminum foil.

While I'd tucked his little sisters into bed, Lukas had tucked himself behind his bedroom door and warned me to stay out because he was working on a big surprise.

But when Mother's Day arrived with dawn's pink streaks and my boy's giddy shrieks, the surprise was all his.

He raced to my bedside with that foil-wrapped box tucked under one arm, and he jumped up and down on the edge of my bed until I flashed him a sleepy smile. As he sang an original rendition of "Happy Mommy's Day to You," I propped myself up on a pillow and let him plop his gift onto my lap.

My 6-year-old watched with wiggly excitement as I oohed and ahhed over the shiny globs of wrapping paper. Little by little, I peeled back those lumpy layers of foil and plucked at the wads of tape until, finally, I lifted a bouquet of brown blooms from that shoebox tomb.

My son's wide blue eyes landed on his gift, and a bewildered grimace replaced his proud grin. But before his disappointment could morph into tears, I pulled Lukas close and thanked him for his thoughtfulness.

Then I hopped out of bed and stuffed those dung-colored daisies into my fanciest crystal vase. And with a wink, I placed that Mother's Day surprise right in the middle of the kitchen table as if it were the perfect centerpiece for our day of celebration.

In hindsight, I realize it was.

I may not have understood it then, but five kids and a dozen years later, I've learned something about motherhood that greeting cards don't acknowledge and brightly colored daisies can't capture.

While motherhood is a beautiful and priceless gift, it is also a surprising summons to die.

And maybe that's why on some days, this high and holy calling feels laborious and lusterless; monotonous and prosaic. Because motherhood (even spiritual motherhood) is more than a mandate to raise the next generation. It is an unending invitation to lay down our lives.

Motherhood is saying no to the clanking cadence of selfishness and yes to the quiet rhythms of love. It's relinquishing pride and persisting in prayer, surrendering greed and growing in grace.

Motherhood is pacing the floor with a crying baby in the dark of night and holding a tearful teen in the depths of disappointment.

Why Every Mom Needs a Bouquet of Dead Flowers

By Alicia Bruxvoort

It's wiping bottoms and noses and floors countless times a day and listening to the same knock-knock joke over and over again.

Motherhood is chasing toddlers when we'd rather be chasing our own dreams. And folding superhero underwear when we'd rather be rescued from the monotony of the daily grind.

Quite simply, motherhood is a daily decision to paint the ordinary moments of our days with the extraordinary love of Christ. And this kind of love may not resemble a bouquet of golden giggles or blossoms of bright pink hugs. It may look more like a batch of brown blooms tucked in a shoebox. Or like our Savior hanging from a rugged cross.

First John 3:16 reminds us that the beauty of true love is always painted with tenacious tints of sacrifice and humble hues of surrender.

Let's be honest: Whether we're moms or wives, daughters or friends, this kind of love doesn't feel easy or natural. But I'm learning that something surprising happens when we fix our eyes on Jesus and follow His example. Little by little, our lives begin to bloom with a beauty that doesn't wilt or wane, falter or fade.

And somehow, as we pour our lives out in love, our faithful Savior uses the gift of daily death to grow us into women radiant with His glory and fully alive in His grace (Psalm 34:5).

What was great today...

_____

_____

What was hard today...

_____

_____

A prayer for my children...

_____

_____

devotional · **hey mama**

Moms: Let's Make This Pledge

By Lysa TerKeurst

"But encourage one another daily, as long as it is called 'Today,' so that none of you may be hardened by sin's deceitfulness." Hebrews 3:13 (NIV)

I really want to be a great mom. I want to raise kids who love the Lord, are respectful, kind, smart and all the other things we want for our kids.

So, I pray. I read parenting books. I teach manners, kiss the skinned knees and help my teen process her first broken heart. I plan the family dinners, the date nights, the vacations. I keep track of who needs what and when. I set the appointments and the discipline parameters and the alarm clock so we can get up and do it all again tomorrow.

And through every minute, I am hyper aware of my frailties and faults.

My heart wants to be incredibly patient and organized and excited about reading books out loud.

But then I get tired. And over-extended. And suddenly my day finds me getting snappy, losing track of all those papers sent home from school and skipping pages to hurry to the end of the book that started off with such promise.

There is a gap between my desires and my reality.

I bet this is true for many moms, so we should all understand those hard places, right? But somewhere in the day-to-day, we can forget how important it is to support each other as moms and sisters in Christ. We can forget the need to foster a sense of community. And as soon as we forget these things, it's much easier for thoughts of judgment to creep in.

In those moments, it's crucial to remember that being a source of encouragement for others is biblical. Our key verse, Hebrews 3:13 tells us to "encourage one another daily" so that we aren't "hardened by sin's deceitfulness" which causes us to unfairly judge others.

So, I was just wondering if we might all make a little pact together today.

A pact to build each other up. To not judge one another. Ever. Even when we parent differently. Even when my kids act like I never taught them manners.

Might you give me the benefit of the doubt? Just assume it's a bad moment, but this isn't an indication of all our moments.

And then I'll give you the benefit of the doubt when your child messes up.

Or when I hear you snap in Target and make threats to your kids that betray every good intention you had that morning. When you prayed. And read the parenting books. And taught manners, kissed skinned knees, planned the dinner, and all the other zillions of things you did so well.

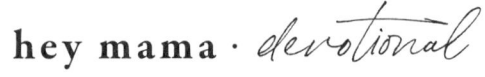

hey mama · *devotional*

Moms: Let's Make This Pledge

By Lysa TerKeurst

Instead of judging you, I will love you.

And maybe you can love me too.

Moms, let's pledge to build each other up instead of tearing each other down. Most of us are desperately trying to do this mothering thing right.

What was great today...
_____
_____

What was hard today...
_____
_____

A prayer for my children...
_____
_____

devotional · **hey mama**

When You're Tired of Coloring in the Lines

By Alicia Bruxvoort

"But he said to me, 'My grace is sufficient for you, for my power is made perfect in weakness.' Therefore I will boast all the more gladly about my weaknesses, so that Christ's power may rest on me."
2 Corinthians 12:9 (NIV)

I was elbow-deep in soapsuds when my 4-year-old's cries prompted me to drop my dishrag and race to the other room. Maggie had been coloring a picture, but when I reached her side, the paper lay crumpled and torn on the floor.

"Honey, what's wrong?" I asked.

"I can't color in the lines," Maggie complained.

I retrieved the wrinkled paper and smoothed it with my palm. The kitty on the coloring page looked like it had been caught in a crossfire.

"See?" my preschooler said, as she rubbed the crayon furiously over the holes on the paper.

I could feel Maggie's frustration as I watched her shoulders tighten with each squiggly stroke. The more she pressed that plum Crayola upon the page, the more the picture ripped beneath her efforts.

"I just can't make anything beautiful," Maggie declared.

What a curious remark from this child who sculpts gourmet cakes from Play-Doh and creates masterpieces on the driveway with a fistful of sidewalk chalk. An artist indeed, my daughter doesn't yet know that beauty isn't always measured between the lines.

Maggie sighed and set down her crayon, and I recognized myself in her try-hard weariness. There, in my 4-year-old's furrowed brow, I saw the mom who had once tried to live within a set of invisible lines.

No one had written out the rules of good parenting for me. They were the result of my own expectations, noble ideas shaped by well-meaning mommy books, fabulous Facebook posts and my personal good-girl gospel.

My lines declared that a good mom keeps a clean house, bakes bread from scratch and arrives everywhere on time. A good mom knows just what to do when her teen slumps into silence, when a toddler refuses to eat her veggies, or when a 6-year-old strings a web of lies.

No matter how hard I tried, my life kept spilling outside the lines.

I was certain that a good mom never lies in bed at night wondering if she is ruining her children. (But sometimes I do.)

A good mom never delivers her child to the wrong soccer field on the wrong day at the wrong time. (But maybe I've done that once or twice.)

And a good mom never leaves the house with dirty-faced children or forgets to pack her kindergartener's lunch. (But I'm guilty of both.)

hey mama · *devotional*

When You're Tired of Coloring in the Lines

By Alicia Bruxvoort

Perhaps you've lived within a self-declared set of lines, too.

Maybe you believe that good wives serve dinner by candlelight and always have the laundry done. Or that good friends always reply to texts and certainly never forget a birthday.

Maybe, like me, the harder you try to live within the lines, the more your soul rips beneath the weight of your efforts.

But here's the good news for try-hard women like us: God's not offended by our flaws and imperfections. God's Word tells us in 2 Corinthians 12:9a, "My grace is sufficient for you, for my power is made perfect in weakness."

That verse was what finally compelled me to trade my invisible lines of expectation for the compassionate contours of my Savior's grace. When I finally stopped obsessing over my flaws and began focusing on His faithfulness, my life took on a new kind of beauty.

Maggie was still crying over the rips in her coloring page, so I tipped her chin and asked her to watch as I placed that picture, holes and all, against the window.

Morning sunbeams streamed right through those holes in the paper and cast a glorious rainbow of light upon the carpet at our feet. Maggie grew quiet staring at the shimmers on the floor and slipped something small and purple into my hand. "I don't need my crayon anymore, Mommy. I like my picture just like that."

So we stood at the window together, watching glory stream through the gaps.

What was great today...

_____
_____

What was hard today...

_____
_____

A prayer for my children...

_____
_____

devotional · **hey mama**

Why Are Women So Hard On Each Other?

By Lynn Cowell

"Do not withhold good from those who deserve it when it's in your power to help them."
Proverbs 3:27 (NLT)

"Why, when a woman walks in a room, do all the other women size her up?" my husband asked.

Where was the nearest rock? I thought, as I desperately wanted to crawl under one. My husband had just pointed out what I've often seen, but didn't think others noticed. Our insecurity tends to come out when we're in situations where we feel "less than" or uncomfortable.

Greg's comment that evening stirred a series of questions in my mind.

What holds us back from offering encouragement when we know most of us struggle with feelings of insecurity?

Why, when we have the power to do so much good for each other, do we not do it?

Why would I not, when I have a good thought about another person, simply say it?

Beautiful comments we think in our head, yet fail to say such as:

"I noticed your kind act in the grocery store. You inspired me!"

"Your generous heart makes me want to be giving as well!"

"When I see the boldness of your faith, I'm encouraged to be bold too."

The more I thought about it, the more I knew how easy it would be to start speaking good things about others.

King Solomon reinforced my thoughts as I read Proverbs 3:27, "Do not withhold good from those who deserve it when it's in your power to help them."

My heart heard a thought from God as I read this verse, "Lynn, do not withhold a compliment. When you speak good, you are doing My good."

So, I'm starting with this resolve: If I have a positive thought, I'm going to say it. It doesn't matter if I know you or if you are a woman I've never met. With God's help, I no longer want to withhold good from those who deserve or those who need it, when it is in my power to help them.

My prayer is that not only will I encourage others along the way, but my kids will see God's goodness pouring through me and they too will be inspired to not withhold good from others. If we'll join together and make sharing the good we see normal, we might just bring some really good change to the world.

Why Are Women So Hard On Each Other?

By Lynn Cowell

What was great today...
_____
_____

What was hard today...
_____
_____

A prayer for my children...
_____
_____

devotional · **hey mama**

end of week 4

What did I learn about God this week?

_____
_____
_____
_____
_____
_____

How can I apply this to motherhood?

_____
_____
_____
_____
_____
_____

week 5

provision

"Consider the ravens: They neither sow nor reap,
they have neither storehouse nor barn, and yet God feeds them.
Of how much more value are you than the birds!"

Luke 12:24

"Do not be frightened, and do not be dismayed, for the LORD your God is with you wherever you go."

Joshua 1:9b

~~I AM ALONE~~

Hope When You're Hanging by a Thread

By Alicia Bruxvoort

"For the word of God is living and active and full of power [making it operative, energizing, and effective] ..." Hebrews 4:12a (AMP)

I never should have done the math.

After all, what good does it do a desperate mama to tally her exhaustion?

Blame it on a mind numbed by years of inconsolable infants or on the sheer monotony of motherhood's daily grind, but for whatever reason, on that starless night long ago, I tried to calculate the number of times I'd foregone a full night's sleep.

Without a doubt, our children are a gift. But each one had come wrapped in colic and wired with wails. And by the time our fourth-born arrived, I was weary beyond words.

We'd read parenting books and consulted doctors, established healthy habits and rhythmic routines, yet nothing changed the fact that our offspring resisted sleep like alley cats skirt puddles.

2,920 days. That's how long it had been since I'd slept through the night. And once I'd quantified my lack, I wanted to cry along with the wee one in my arms.

Deep down, I knew that my discouragement wasn't the result of sleepless nights alone. My body was exhausted, but my heart was depleted as well.

I'd been hanging by a thread for so long I couldn't even pray. I knew God was with me, but I couldn't find the words to tell Him what I needed.

Perhaps you've been there, too — worn out and worn down, wordless and weary. Maybe you're there right now. Sleep-deprived moms aren't the only ones who know the ache of a sapped soul.

Anyone who is stretched thin or poured out, distressed or discouraged, is likely to taste its anguish too.

"God, I know You're here," I whispered into the dark. "But I don't know what to say ..."

That's when I noticed the Bible within reach of the rocking chair where I sat. Careful not to jostle the baby on my lap, I grabbed God's Word and flipped through the pages.

Eventually, my tired eyes fell on Hebrews 4:12a — "For the word of God is living and active and full of power [making it operative, energizing, and effective] ..."

As that verse sank deep, a hushed hope began to rise. Perhaps I was holding God's answer to my weary cries.

My soul felt sapped, but God's Word was alive and active.

My body felt weak, but God's Word was full of power.

My mind felt fatigued, but God's Word was energizing.

My efforts felt fruitless, but God's Word was operative and effective.

Hope When You're Hanging by a Thread

By Alicia Bruxvoort

So, 2,920 days after my last full night of sleep, I began a new midnight routine. When the house grew quiet and the baby whimpered loud, I opened my Bible and declared its timeless truth.

Sometimes I chose one verse and spoke it aloud until my sagging spirit echoed, "Yes!" Sometimes I proclaimed the promises of Jesus until my haggard heart was buoyed with hope. Sometimes I sang a psalm until my mind's downcast rap was replaced by a refrain of praise.

I didn't have the strength to reach out for my Savior, but I let the truth of His Word reach the depths of my weary soul. I didn't have the energy to create powerful prayers, but I turned God's Word into personal pleas. And slowly, surely, my desperation turned to peace. My circumstances hadn't changed, but something within me had.

I was still stretched, but I was no longer sinking.

I was still poured out, but I was no longer empty.

I was still fatigued, but I was no longer frazzled.

One night as I sat in that rocking chair and murmured God's Word above my baby's bellows, I realized this — I was no longer holding on to God's promises; God's promises were holding on to me.

That's the wonder of God's Word, dear friends. It sustains us and supports us. It restores us and remakes us. And when we take hold of its truth, the Truth holds us, too.

Even when we're hanging by a thread. Especially when we're hanging by a thread.

What was great today...

_____

_____

What was hard today...

_____

_____

A prayer for my children...

_____

_____

devotional · **hey mama**

If God Really Loved Me

By Lysa TerKeurst

"'Though the mountains be shaken and the hills be removed, yet my unfailing love for you will not be shaken nor my covenant of peace be removed,' says the LORD, who has compassion on you." Isaiah 54:10 (NIV)

I wonder what would happen in our lives if we really lived in the absolute assurance of God's love. I mean, as Christians we know He loves us. We sing the songs, we quote the verses, we wear the T-shirts and we sport the bumper stickers. Yes, God loves us.

I'm not talking about knowing He loves us.

I'm talking about living as if we really believe it.

I'm talking about walking confidently in the certainty of God's love even when our feelings beg us not to.

I'm talking about training our hearts and our minds to process everything through the filter of the absolute assurance of God's love. Period. Without the possible question mark.

Not too long ago, I had a conversation with a precious mom whose eldest daughter is nearing 30 and has never had a boyfriend. The younger siblings have all gone through the whole dating thing, and one is engaged to be married. The eldest daughter sat on the side of her mom's bed recently with tears slipping down her cheeks and asked, "Why, Mom? Why can't I find anyone to love me? What's wrong with me?"

This mom was asking me for advice in helping her daughter process these questions. These feelings are real. These feelings are tough.

And I'm sure if I were able to untangle all the emotions wrapped in and around these questions, somewhere deep inside I would find this girl doubting God's love for her.

I completely understand. In my own life, I have faced heartbreaking situations where I know God could step in and change everything in an instant. And when He doesn't? It hurts. Deeply.

But here is what God continues to teach me — I must process disappointments through the filter of His love, not through the tangled places of my heart.

When I process things through the tangled places of my heart, often the outcome is, "If God loves me so much, why would He let this happen?"

Instead, when I process things through the filter of the absolute assurance of God's love, the outcome is, "God loves me so much; therefore I have to trust why He is allowing this to happen."

I took the mom's hand who was asking for advice and told her to help her daughter rewrite the way she is processing this. It's okay to feel hurt, lonely and sad. But these feelings shouldn't be a trigger to doubt God's love for her. They should be a trigger to look for God's protection, provision and possible growth opportunities.

If God Really Loved Me

By Lysa TerKeurst

I know this can be hard. But what if we really lived in the absolute assurance of God's love? Oh sweet sister, in whatever you are facing today, I pray Isaiah 54:10a over you, "Though the mountains be shaken and the hills be removed, yet [God's] unfailing love for you will not be shaken."

What was great today...
_____
_____

What was hard today...
_____
_____

A prayer for my children...
_____
_____

devotional · **hey mama**

The Uncomfortable Gift of Elbow Room

By Amy Carroll

"He brought me out into a spacious place; he rescued me because he delighted in me." Psalm 18:19 (NIV)

Like a door slamming behind me, the long, happy season of life ended abruptly. I suddenly found myself in new territory. At first, the space around me felt hollow and echo-y and bare.

I was scared because the place I had occupied for so long was familiar and safe. It was a place where I knew the rules and benefited from support, so moving into a new space was filled with the dread of the unknown.

I was hurt because the shift felt like a rejection. Mouths that were once filled with a "yes" now spoke "no."

Change can be terrifying, right?

But strangely, I was excited too. Even though I felt like a baby bird pushed out of the nest, facing empty space was my opportunity to fly. I was uncertain, but the air around me was fresh and clear.

I needed to head into the new season with a fresh perspective. Psalm 18:19 provided the perfect words to express a positive shift. "He brought me out into a spacious place; he rescued me because he delighted in me." Examining the parts of this divine piece of poetry helped me see things in a different light.

"He brought me out …"

I'm not completely change-resistant, but I'm definitely change-reluctant. Most of us prefer stability to change, yet God grants us all "bringing out" stages of life.

There's the career woman who's brought out of the workplace to stay at home, and the stay-at-home mom who returns to work.

The college student who moves into the adulting life of paychecks and bills.

The woman who exchanges the title of "wife" for "widow."

The mother who trades the dream of childbirth with the one of choosing to enfold another mother's child.

The divorcee who creates a happy life that she didn't choose.

Change is tough, but we can trust that God is in the midst of it. He alone has the power to bring us out.

"Into a spacious place …"

New places, titles and circumstances give us elbow room and leave space for growth no matter whether they're chosen or given. The strangeness of the unknown is uncomfortable, but it's a room in which we can mature.

In my change, I wasn't dependent on one network anymore (although we remained fast friends!), but I gained new connections that expanded my opportunities more than I ever imagined. I grieved a loss but also found joy in my spacious new location.

"He rescued me …"

The Uncomfortable Gift of Elbow Room

By Amy Carroll

If you're like change-reluctant me, God has often given me a kind shove since He knows I may never jump! His nudge may feel like bruising at first, but I can always look back and see that it was a rescue. He saves us from stagnancy and immaturity by rescuing us from being stuck.

Change is hard because it always involves a loss, but our good God makes sure that there are gains that accompany our grief.

"Because He delighted in me."

The shift I experienced was painful for a moment, but the benefits and joy I've experienced in my new, spacious place have exponentially exceeded the pain. Change created exciting opportunities, new connections and greater personal maturity.

God delights in me, and He delights in you too. His heart of love for us means we can trust that His changes in our lives will always be worked for our good. (See Romans 8:28.)

When change feels scary, I invite you into a perspective shift with me. Look at the new, increased space around you. It is elbow room filled with God's love and provision. He's there with you, moving with You into fresh territory.

What was great today...

_____

_____

What was hard today...

_____

_____

A prayer for my children...

_____

_____

devotional · **hey mama**

Three Things Every Mom Should Know

By Lysa TerKeurst

"Finally, be strong in the Lord and in his mighty power." Ephesians 6:10 (NIV)

Being a mom is a high honor and one of the most precious gifts of my life. At the same time, being a mom is tough.

It's tough when your children are tiny. And there are still tough days when you're like me, and your children are all grown.

One of the hardest things about motherhood for me has always been my tendency to blame myself for the wrong choices my kids have made.

The second hardest thing is trying to figure out the right way to help them navigate their issues. Especially when you're hyper aware that the situation your child is in carries great consequences.

Deep is the sorrow of a mother who feels helpless.

Thankfully, God knows what it's like to deal with wayward children. He feels our pain. He knows our sorrow. And He knows exactly how to encourage us through His Word.

Ephesians 6:10-12 tells us: "Finally, be strong in the Lord and in his mighty power. Put on the full armor of God so you can take your stand against the devil's schemes. For our struggle is not against flesh and blood but against the rulers, against the authorities, against the powers of this dark world and against the spiritual forces of evil in the heavenly realms." (NIV)

Based on this truth, here are three things mamas should know:

1. God does not call us to find a power within ourselves to overcome the issues we face with our kids.

He calls us to put on His armor because what we are facing is a battle of epic proportions. And His weapons aren't silly little spiritual suggestions that might or might not work. His weapons are certain.

His belt of truth. I must park my runaway mind in the assurance of God's love for me and my child.

His breastplate of righteousness. I must stop reacting in the flesh and choose to battle this with my praises and prayers.

His gospel of peace. I must walk in the assurance and peace that even when I can't see things changing, God is working on my child's behalf.

His shield of faith. I must have faith in God's timing and His ways.

His helmet of salvation. I must trust God's ultimate desire for my children is for them to have a close relationship with Him. Though a situation might seem like an unlikely part of this process, God will bring good out of it.

His sword, which is the Bible. I must read God's love letter to me every day. And hold those truths as the lifeline between God's security and my shaky heart.

His gift of prayer. I must see prayer not as a last resort but as the very thing God's most courageous warriors turn to first.

Ephesians 6:13-18 assures us that with these in place, we'll be able to stand as we use them to tap into a power beyond ourselves.

hey mama · devotional

Three Things Every Mom Should Know

By Lysa TerKeurst

2. The battle isn't against our child and their choices.

It often feels like the battle is against our child. In reality, the battle is against Satan's schemes.

There will be some battles we face with our kids that seem impossible to win because Satan twists the truth. He hides consequences. He blinds reality. He has schemes perfectly designed with our weaknesses in mind.

Therefore, we have to battle Satan. He's the real enemy here. And because we are Jesus girls, we hold the power for victory in our praises and prayers to God.

3. The battle is taking place in the heavenly realms.

Oh how I want to fight my kids' battles with what I can see. But that simply isn't enough.

So, I must fight with the only thing I have that can reach into the heavenly realm: my praise and prayers. Praise for who God is and prayers for Him to remove Satan's influence in a situation.

If ever I'm tempted to doubt how powerful praise and prayers are in battle, a quick read of 2 Chronicles 20:1-27 soothes this mama's heart. It's an amazing story of God's people feeling overwhelmed in the face of a vast army, but when they begin to sing and praise the Lord, their enemy is defeated.

Prayers to God and praises for God release the power of God.

What bridged the gap between them feeling powerless and experiencing victory were praises and prayers. And it's the same for us.

I can't fully explain it. But I can proclaim it. Our prayers and our praises are powerful and effective.

Yes, being a mom is tough, but we aren't alone. God understands this struggle of parenting children who get off track.

And since God, the perfect parent, has dealt with this since the beginning of time — I think His is the best advice around.

What was great today...

What was hard today...

A prayer for my children...

devotional · **hey mama**

I Don't Know If I Can Do This

By Katy McCown

"This is a catalog of the kings of the land whom Joshua and the Israelites defeated ... 31 kings in all." Joshua 12:7a, 24b (VOICE)

I didn't really want to keep watching, but for some reason I couldn't stop.

A real-life tightrope walker dared to cross a gorge near the Grand Canyon on live television. I didn't know this man, but my fear for him and his potential plummet to the bottom of the canyon was real. With each step I prayed, Please God, let him make it across!

The wind blew so hard at times he'd stop and squat on the rope to lower himself beneath the gusts. He would pause and pray, then stand and continue across.

Yet possibly the craziest part was this wasn't his first attempt at something so risky.

If I ever crossed a canyon, or a waterfall, or something else really high on a tight-rope and I survived, let me assure you — that would be the first and only time you'd see me do such a thing.

Stepping out of our comfort zones can be scary. But to do it more than once takes true faith. That's the kind of faith the Israelites had. We see this especially as they conquered the Promised Land.

In our key verse, we read "This is a catalog of the kings of the land whom Joshua and the Israelites defeated ..." (Joshua 12:7a). The chapter ends with "... 31 kings in all." Tucked between these verses, we find the names of kings in the land of Canaan who fought, but couldn't defeat, Joshua and God's people as they entered the land God promised them.

After the walls of Jericho fell, the army marched, God moved in power and the Israelite army conquered 30 more kings.

And I wonder, with each new foe: Did they worry about the outcome? Did they question if God would show up this time like He did that day at Jericho?

Too often, I march into daily battles, wondering if this will be the time God doesn't show up, rather than charging full speed ahead, knowing Whom I'm following and counting fully on Him.

Like the time I sat behind the wheel of my van with a long drive ahead. I'd made this drive many times; however, this time, I faced the road as the sole adult in the car with all six of my kids.

Enter fear, panic, doubt, maybe even a few tears.

But before I fell completely over the edge, God interrupted. He reminded me of prayer and my direct access to Him at all times. He pointed me to the many times He'd provided and counseled me to count on Him again.

So instead of wondering if God would show up, I threw all my concerns on His shoulders. Dear God, help us go the whole way without one stop. Help no one have to use the bathroom. Help the kids not fight. Help the traffic keep moving. Help me not get tired. Help no one get hungry.

hey mama · *devotional*

I Don't Know If I Can Do This

By Katy McCown

I've heard confidence defined as "demonstrated ability." And I think we can apply this definition to our spiritual lives.

I don't know how Joshua and his army approached each battle following the victory at Jericho, but I know how they should have — confidently. God had demonstrated His ability at Jericho (and many other times, too).

This same confidence is available to us through Jesus. When we make Jesus Lord of our lives, God is not only with us, He is also in us. And since God is able, and God is with us, we can count on Him.

As the man on the tightrope crouched beneath the winds, one thing changed everything. Across the canyon, his father spoke into a microphone linked to an earpiece that fed directly into his son's soul.

The son walked, as the father talked.

The father encouraged, supported and guided. Another step. He cheered, comforted and listened. Another step. No matter how hard the wind blew, the son knew his father saw him, and he heard his father say, "You can do this."

And just like that father and son, God walked me down my road, guiding me and my car full of kids safely from one place to another.

Is it time for you to step out on the tightrope of trust?

What was great today...

_____

_____

What was hard today...

_____

_____

A prayer for my children...

_____

_____

devotional · **hey mama**

Strength for Your Struggle

By Micca Campbell

"And He said to me, 'My grace is sufficient for you, for My strength is made perfect in weakness.' Therefore most gladly I will rather boast in my infirmities, that the power of Christ may rest upon me."
2 Corinthians 12:9 (NKJV)

Being a single parent when my son was young was difficult on many levels. Most of the time I felt tired and overwhelmed by all my responsibilities. There was no one to share concerns with—no one to worry with, plan with, or give a bath to my son when I needed a break.

To make matters worse, we lived in an upstairs duplex. When my son was a baby, it was a challenge getting him, his diaper bag and the groceries upstairs at the same time. I didn't want to leave him in the house or the car alone so I piled on the items. Once I climbed to the top of the stairs, my next challenge was unlocking the door with my arms filled to overflowing.

Most days I felt like the whole world rested on my shoulders. While I tried to carry the load, I was too weak. It was crushing me, and yet, I continued to fight. I tried harder. I had to. I had to be strong. If I put down the load, who was going to pick it up?

One day, I came across our key verse: "My grace is sufficient for you, for My strength is made perfect in weakness." Hope awoke in my heart when I realized my situation was an avenue to experience God's strength. I didn't have to put on a brave face, or pretend to be made of steel. I simply needed to surrender my weaknesses to God in exchange for His strength.

This is what Paul did in 2 Corinthians 12:7-10. He prayed repeatedly about a difficult situation in his life, asking the Lord to take it from him. God responded, "My grace is sufficient."

I discovered God answered me in the same way He did Paul when I shared my struggles with Him. God didn't expect me to parent alone, but gave me His strength in my weaknesses. He promised, "that the power of Christ may rest upon me" (2 Corinthians 12:9). That promise is yours, too.

An interesting way to view His power is by taking a look at this verse in it's original Greek. The word "rest" literally means "a tent or covering." Christ's power over our circumstances and in our weaknesses is a shelter in which to rest, take refuge from the storms, and is our protective covering.

God's grace—His loving-kindness, joy, and strength—was enough for Paul, and it's enough for you and me.

When I began praying to God about my situation asking for help, my circumstances didn't change right away. But I had a renewed sense of God's presence and power in my life, and no longer felt alone. Through the assistance of others, I began to see God's activity in the life of my son and me. He had always been there offering help. I just needed to swallow my pride and receive it. When I let my friend cut my grass and the teenager next door play with my son so I could do household chores, I felt equipped to press on with all the other challenges of daily life.

Strength for Your Struggle

By Micca Campbell

That's not all. Paul not only surrendered his struggles to God, but he had a positive attitude as well: "I will rather boast in my infirmities, that the power of Christ may rest upon me" (2 Corinthians 12:9).

Looking for and acknowledging God's strength in my weakness was better for my attitude than grumbling. Complaining was a dead end. However, boasting in what God can do in me infused my faith, causing me to depend on His strength more and more. His promise became a reality in my life. For when I am weak, He is strong!

In facing our struggles and fears, it's vital that we yield completely to God. When we do, God can use our burdens as an avenue for His power and grace.

What was great today…

_____

_____

What was hard today…

_____

_____

A prayer for my children…

_____

_____

devotional · **hey mama**

end of week 5

What did I learn about God this week?

_____
_____
_____
_____
_____
_____

How can I apply this to motherhood?

_____
_____
_____
_____
_____
_____

hey mama · *devotional*

week 6

purpose

"And we know that for those who love God
all things work together for good,
for those who are called according to his purpose."

Romans 8:28

"For it is God who works in you to will and to act in order to fulfill his good purpose."

PHILIPPIANS 2:13

~~I CAN'T MAKE AN IMPACT FOR THE KINGDOM~~

Why I No Longer Cry Over Burnt Bread

By Alicia Bruxvoort

"Whatever you do, work heartily, as for the Lord and not for men." Colossians 3:23 (ESV)

I was squashed between kindergarteners in the school cafeteria when my 6-year-old son, Joshua, made an announcement that gave me the giggles. I hid my mouth behind a napkin to cover my smirk and realized that at one point in my life, my son's innocent words would have spawned tears instead of chuckles.

It started when the little boy next to me lifted a sandwich out of his lunch box.

"That's huge!" Joshua exclaimed as he poked at the lukewarm carrots on his cafeteria tray and gazed longingly at his classmate's lunch.

The sandwich was big. Oversized slabs of cheese and slices of ham nestled between two thick slices of bread. I wondered how much cash it would take to talk a kindergartner into trading his mealtime masterpiece for my soggy sloppy joe.

"Can you even get that in your mouth?" I teased as my lunch companion freed his sandwich from plastic wrap and lifted the culinary sensation to his mouth.

"I'm used to big bread," he replied. "It's my mom's specialty."

Joshua raised an eyebrow and studied the specimen in his classmate's hands. "You mean your mom makes the bread you eat?"

The little fellow nodded happily.

My son looked at me with wide-eyed wonder, then shrugged his shoulders and replied, "Oh, my mom's specialty is burnt bread."

I nodded in agreement. "If the crust's not charred, the bread's not ours," I said with a laugh.

The sandwich muncher beside me didn't even blink at my corny rhyme, but Joshua applauded me with a big smile.

Soon a bell announced the lunch hour's end, and the kindergarteners hurried to line up for recess. My brown-haired boy waved and marched off to the playground, leaving me alone with my speckled pink cafeteria tray, a mound of lukewarm carrots and a smile.

A decade ago my young son's honesty would have left me feeling second-rate. I would have raced to the library to check out a book on baking homemade bread.

I've learned the hard way that I miss all sorts of sacred and significant moments when I live with the frantic insistence that I can do it all. When I'm striving to be good at all things, I miss the joy of small things.

A good mom isn't good at everything. She's just really good at one thing. A good mom is good at being who God created her to be.

hey mama · devotional

Why I No Longer Cry Over Burnt Bread

By Alicia Bruxvoort

The truth for bread-burning mamas like me sitting in school cafeterias and for gifted women like you sitting in mini-vans, corporate offices and rocking chairs is this: We weren't created to do it all.

We were created to play one small role in a gigantic Kingdom tale. And if we spend our lives trying to mimic everyone else's script, we might miss the lines that are uniquely ours.

On any given day, I can tell you a few things I do well. But, perhaps more importantly, I can tell you what I don't do.

I learned a few years ago the importance of creating a list of what I don't do. If you're tired of feeling tired, make that list. If you're worn out from the comparison game, make that list. If you can't celebrate your talents and laugh at your limitations, make that list.

Stick it to your bathroom mirror. Carry it in your purse. And refuse to apologize for being you.

So, friend, if you've been made to bake homemade bread, by all means, bake away.

If you've been fashioned to encourage others, speak life.

If you've been gifted to sing, fill the earth with music, please.

But whatever you do, don't try to do it all, or you just might miss the one thing that the world desperately needs you to do.

What was great today…

_____
_____

What was hard today…

_____
_____

A prayer for my children…

_____
_____

devotional · **hey mama**

Cleaning Up a Mess I Didn't Make

By Chrystal Evans Hurst

"And I pray that you ... grasp how wide and long and high and deep is the love of Christ ..."
Ephesians 3:17b-18 (NIV)

When my middle son was 2 years old, he went through various stages that almost sent me to the mad house.

One of the most irritating stages was his habit of taking off his diaper after putting him to bed. Many late nights we would have to put on a fresh diaper, change his sheets and put him back to bed.

After awhile, we wised up. We started putting him into all-in-one pajamas that made it not so easy for him to accomplish his little feat.

That pretty much solved the problem.

Until one night, when my husband put the boys (ages 2 and 4) to bed. Unfortunately, he forgot about our precautionary measure of locking our toddler into his diaper.

Before long, our eldest son shouted at the top of his lungs, "Mommy! It stinks in here! Somebody needs his diaper changed!"

No worries. It happens, right?

Soon we heard urgency in our eldest son's voice as he called out again, "MOMMY! COME QUICK! THERE'S A STINKY MESS IN HERE!"

We entered their room. The smell that greeted me at the door was enough to make me want to run for my life.

Friends, we are talking yuck e-v-e-r-y-w-h-e-r-e ... on the sheets, blankets, feet and smudged into the carpet.

So that night, while many other mothers slept peacefully in their beds, guess what I was doing?

Cleaning up a mess.

At almost midnight and for close to an hour, I was on my hands and knees cleaning and scrubbing. I'll spare you the gory details.

Believe it or not, the carpet today looks like nothing ever happened. Between my cleaning concoctions that fateful night and a borrowed steam cleaner the next day, I managed to handle the situation like a pro.

Of course I did. I'm a mom. That's what moms do. We clean up after our children when necessary, because that's what love does.

There is a lesson to be learned from the middle of this messy situation ...

My son didn't mean to make a mess. He didn't intentionally deprive me of sleep or aim to make me uncomfortable. He didn't mean to make me suffer for his transgression.

But I did.

And why? Because that's what love does.

hey mama · devotional

Cleaning Up a Mess I Didn't Make

By Chrystal Evans Hurst

Even when he wasn't showing me much love, I loved him anyway. And I showed my love by cleaning up a mess that I didn't make.

My dear sister... don't you know Jesus loves us this same way?

He saw us in our mess. He cleaned up after us. He was willing to suffer for our transgressions. And even when we aren't showing Him much love, He loved us first and continues to love us anyway.

Because that's what love does.

I believe with all my heart that as my son matures, he will be grateful and appreciate my sacrifices. I pray that eventually he will come to understand the width, length, height and depth of the love I have for him. Just like God's love for us, Paul prayed that the church at Ephesus "may have power, together with all the Lord's holy people, to grasp how wide and long and high and deep is the love of Christ" (Ephesians 3:18).

In the same way, as we mature in our relationship with God and develop a greater understanding of why we needed His rescue, we can appreciate more and more His huge sacrifice.

Here's the kicker – our lives, actions and attitudes should show it.

Just like mothers find a way to do what seems

... inconceivable

... impossible

... or insurmountable ...

so, too, our precious Savior found a way to rescue us from our plight.

And I'm so thankful. Aren't you?

What was great today...

What was hard today...

A prayer for my children...

devotional · **hey mama**

Worth the Effort

By Lynn Cowell

"The purposes of a person's heart are deep waters, but one who has insight draws them out."
Proverbs 20:5 (NIV)

There are two kinds of young women who live in my house. One speaks her mind freely; you don't have to guess where she stands or how she feels. The other is more reserved, holding her emotions and words in check.

Neither one is right or wrong. Both are deep thinkers and deep feelers. Yet my girls couldn't be more different when it comes to how their thoughts and emotions are expressed. With one, I have a sense of her constant pulse as she daily shares her joys and struggles. With the other ... well, as my mother used to say about my father, "Still waters run deep."

The writer of Proverbs 20:5 encourages us to make the effort to "draw out" people. As I have found with my daughter, there is much beauty and young wisdom in the deep well of her heart. And while it takes extra work to tap into that low-lying spring, it is often rewarded.

In a culture where our conversations are often capped at 140 characters on Twitter or summed up in two or three sentences on Facebook or text messaging, real conversation may be in jeopardy. The days of front porches and Sunday dinners seem to be all but gone. Yet God's Word tells us a person's heart is deep waters—not something simple and concise that can be summed up short and sweet.

Whether it is with our daughters, neighbors or girlfriends, we need unhurried moments to draw from each other's hearts. We need time to listen to the wisdom and work God is accomplishing in another's life. These types of conversations usually don't develop in a quick greeting of "How are you?" as we're moving from one task to another. But more often, they are in the intentional moments when we propose to listen.

In the original Hebrew language of the Old Testament, "purposes" in this verse means advice, counsel, and plans. Many times, when we take time to listen, we can discover plans our friend has tucked away in her heart. Sometimes it will mean realizing her hidden hope of visiting prisoners and sharing the Gospel with them. Or you might discover your child is reading the Bible on her own as she shares a verse she found.

Drawing out another or engaging in purposeful conversation also helps us gain insight, wisdom, hope and encouragement when we listen to all God is doing in their heart. We can receive advice and counsel simply by listening to one of His children.

Stop right now and look at your calendar. Pick a time—tonight, tomorrow or this weekend, and invite someone dear to you to spend time with. Whether it is your daughter whose life spins in and out of your home, or that girlfriend you haven't had coffee with in months, be intentional. Send her a text, give her a call, just make sure to make time. And to listen to the deep waters of her heart.

Worth the Effort

By Lynn Cowell

What was great today...
_____
_____

What was hard today...
_____
_____

A prayer for my children...
_____
_____

devotional · **hey mama**

The Most Important Lesson

By Lysa TerKeurst

"Fix these words of mine in your hearts and minds; tie them as symbols on your hands and bind them on your foreheads. Teach them to your children, talking about them when you sit at home and when you walk along the road, when you lie down and when you get up." Deuteronomy 11:18-19 (NIV)

Early in my motherhood adventure I realized I could solve my kids' problems for them. Not every problem. But for the most part, when they had an issue, I could step in and be the solution.

Or ...

I had another option. I could mentor and equip my kids to solve their issues. This approach is much more time consuming, brain draining, and sometimes quite frustrating.

But for me, the most important lesson I want to teach my kids is how to think.

It's that whole "give a man a fish" thing. Give him a fish and he'll eat for a day ... or teach him to fish and he'll eat for a lifetime.

I don't want to train my children to always turn to me for solutions. I want them to learn to think in biblically and emotionally healthy ways and process life's choices in grounded, mature ways. Eventually, they will become solution finders.

If I only tell my kids what they can and can't do, I'm establishing rules for them to follow. This is a part of parenting for sure, but it can't be the whole part.

If I teach them how to think, I'm establishing healthy processing patterns that will serve them when they're no longer under my immediate watch.

For example, texting while driving is deadly. I've taught them this rule. But to help them learn to process the dangers of driving while distracted, I decided to have a family discussion.

Recently, I asked each of the kids to come to a scheduled family dinner equipped to present a brief report on the dangers of texting and driving.

As they presented their reports, I saw the light bulbs coming on in their thought processes. They weren't just learning a rule; they were discovering how to think about this dangerous habit. They were passionate about it. And the best part? They independently committed to not text and drive.

They owned it. Not because I preached a rule at them. But rather, because I helped them learn how to think through this danger for themselves.

The Bible instructs us to teach our kids the truths of God by talking and processing with them all throughout the day. Obviously, texting and driving isn't a biblical truth, but how powerful it is to apply a Biblical mindset to every issue we face.

The Most Important Lesson

By Lysa TerKeurst

So, be it a Scriptural truth or processing life stuff in general, I think the secret is tucked within the beautiful words of our key verse, Deuteronomy 11:18-21 (NIV):

"Fix these words of mine in your hearts and minds; tie them as symbols on your hands and bind them on your foreheads. Teach them to your children, talking about them when you sit at home and when you walk along the road, when you lie down and when you get up. Write them on the doorframes of your houses and on your gates, so that your days and the days of your children may be many …"

Yes, may our days together be many. Learning. Thinking. And processing each problem through the filter of God's Truth.

What was great today...

_____

_____

What was hard today...

_____

_____

A prayer for my children...

_____

_____

devotional · **hey mama**

The Micromanaging Mama
By Karen Ehman

"Don't let your spirit rush to be angry, for anger abides in the heart of fools." Ecclesiastes 7:9 (HCSB)

I couldn't think of anything more exciting than going to Sylvia's house for the afternoon. She had fancy clothes and the neighborhood's only built-in swimming pool. But best of all?

Sylvia had one amazing dollhouse.

There were bedroom sets with dressers, cloth curtains in the windows, and colorful spreads on the beds. There was a living room set with a tiny television and a kitchen with real-looking appliances in the trendy shade of turquoise.

To top it all off, it came with a family — pliable, lifelike miniature human beings who smiled no matter how I posed them. There was even a trusty canine I named Scrappy.

I could arrange the furniture any way I desired. The petite pots and pans were just the way I liked on the stove to simmer. The baby woke up from her nap just when I wanted. The family members entered and exited on my cue. No object missed a single prompt in the scenarios that played out at the ends of my chubby little fingertips.

However, my perfect little world was easily shattered. Sometimes, when I had to go home to eat dinner, Sylvia wanted to play with her own toys. Later I'd return to find the house rearranged by someone who was not going along with my program.

I never liked when someone messed with my plan. In fact, it made me angry.

Today my days still revolve around a house. The furniture is bigger. The dishes and rugs are real. The people are too. And I still don't like anyone messing with my plan.

Messing with my plan often looks like this: abandoned dirty dishes, shoes scattered haphazardly, newly washed windows dotted with sticky fingerprints, mud tracked floors, crumbs trailed, trash not taken out as asked, homework undone, pokey kids making the family late for church. Again.

And sadly, messing with my plan can also find me behaving like this: sharp words strategically hurled, a caustic demeanor meant to snap my family to attention, or a "martyr mom" pose I suddenly strike to convey my "I-do-so-much-for-all-of-you-people-and-what-thanks-do-I-get?" message.

At times like this, as today's key verse from Ecclesiastes 7:9 states, my spirit rushes to anger. When anger takes the lead, I can go from mild-mannered mother to micromanaging mama in three seconds flat to try and make my family "get with the program—and PRONTO!"

Rushing to anger in an attempt to micromanage can lead to hurt feelings, crumpled spirits and fractured relationships in need of repair. Of course we should expect our children to do as they are asked, to perform their chores or remember their school responsibilities.

The Micromanaging Mama

By Karen Ehman

But, when they don't — because they are kids and like us, not perfect — how will we choose to behave? Do we choose to be like Jesus, who would respond appropriately and with self-control, or like a wild woman who somehow thinks yelling is effective although it has never, ever worked in the past.

Will you join me in a challenge to pause before pouncing? To not rush to anger and instead rush to Jesus' side? It is there we can allow Jesus to temper our tempers and filter our words so we can behave in a way that honors Him—and our family members too.

What was great today...

_____
_____

What was hard today...

_____
_____

A prayer for my children...

_____
_____

devotional · **hey mama**

The Leading Role
By Glynnis Whitwer

"Listen, my son, to your father's instruction and do not forsake your mother's teaching." Proverbs 1:8 (NIV)

When our third son was born, the balance of power shifted in our family. My husband and I were outnumbered and the three little blue-blankets knew it. Every day it seemed a conspiracy was afoot to make me slightly bonkers.

I devoured parenting books but usually slapped them down on the coffee table in disgust. The authors offered great advice, but not one told me what to do when three little boys were misbehaving in three different ways at exactly the same time.

Was I the first mother in the history of the world to have this situation?

Frustration at my inability to get things under control increased daily. Why couldn't I manage my children? I had been successful in my career, scored high in leadership on several spiritual gifts tests and easily led others in clubs or organizations.

So what happened? Where was my initiative? My influence? Rather than a leader to follow, my boys saw a frazzled woman with no vision. No wonder they weren't lining up to obey.

And there I was feeling like a prisoner with three little wardens. I had relinquished my authority and was simply trying to survive.

The day finally came when I decided to make a change. It was the day I realized motherhood is another opportunity to lead. Proverbs 1:8 reminded me that God had called me to instruct, teach and lead my boys, not the other way around!

The more I thought about it, the more excited I became. It energized me to consider motherhood as a leadership role. And I longed to learn more.

Yet I was also concerned about usurping the authority of Jesus and my husband in my children's lives. Each day I prayerfully asked God to help me live within His hierarchy of honor and respect while showing me how to effectively lead my children.

I was desperate for direction and wisdom from God, which meant lots of time in His Word seeking to understand my position in Christ and as a mom.

It meant reminding myself on those really hard days, "I am the mother, I am the mother."

It also meant leading and modeling the behavior I wanted to see in them, rather than pouting, which is what I often felt like doing. And oh my, is this hard.

Leading as a mother is particularly difficult given the dailiness of it. Plus my emotional responses aren't always logical. So when I get worn down with challenges and disappointments, I'm tempted to let my children lead. Rather than setting the bar high, I think about lowering it just to get through the day.

The Leading Role
By Glynnis Whitwer

Sometimes I do. Sometimes I give in when I should stand strong. And in those moments of weakness I've discovered God's grace is there for me ... especially then. For it's in the weakest moments of my parenting that God has seemed the closest. And knowing He's there for me gives me courage to try again.

Since those hard early years, God added two little girls to our family through adoption and those little boys are now 20, 18 and 16. I truly love teaching and instructing my kids. Since those hard early years, God add two daughters to our family through adoption, and now they're all grown.

Leading my children is the hardest job I've ever tackled. The costs have been high. But for the young adults who call me "Mom," it's a price I'm willing to pay.

What was great today...

_____

_____

What was hard today...

_____

_____

A prayer for my children...

_____

_____

devotional · **hey mama**

end of week 6

What did I learn about God this week?

_____
_____
_____
_____
_____
_____

How can I apply this to motherhood?

_____
_____
_____
_____
_____
_____

hey mama · *devotional*

additional notes

additional notes

ABOUT PROVERBS 31 MINISTRIES

Know the Truth. Live the Truth. It changes everything.

If you were inspired by *Hey Mama: In Christ, You Are More Than Enough*, and desire to deepen your own personal relationship with Jesus Christ, Proverbs 31 Ministries has just what you are looking for.

Proverbs 31 Ministries exists to be a trusted friend who will take you by the hand and walk by your side, leading you one step closer to the heart of God through:

- Free daily devotions.
- First 5 Bible study app.
- Online Bible Studies.
- Proverbs 31 Podcast.
- COMPEL Writers Training.
- She Speaks Conference.
- Books and resources.

Our desire is to help you to know the Truth and live the Truth. Because when you do, it changes everything.

For more information about Proverbs 31 Ministries, visit: proverbs31.org.

encouragement for today

DAILY DEVOTIONS

WHAT DOES THE BIBLE SAY ABOUT WHAT YOU'RE GOING THROUGH?

SUBSCRIBE TO OUR FREE **ENCOURAGEMENT FOR TODAY** DAILY DEVOTIONS TO RECEIVE DAILY, BIBLICAL ENCOURAGEMENT THAT WILL HELP YOU FILTER EVERYDAY LIFE THROUGH THE TRUTH OF GOD'S WORD.

Go to proverbs31.org/read/devotions to sign up for free!